D0224704

THE OPEN CONSPIRACY

Recent Titles in
Praeger Studies on the 21st Century

THE OPEN CONSPIRACY

H.G. Wells
on
World Revolution

Edited and with a

Critical Introduction

by W. Warren Wagar

Praeger Studies on the 21st Century

PRAEGER

Westport, Connecticut
London

Library of Congress Cataloging-in-Publication Data

Wells, H. G. (Herbert George), 1866–1946.
    The open conspiracy : H.G. Wells on world revolution / edited and with a critical introduction by W. Warren Wagar.
        p.   cm.—(Praeger Studies on the 21st century, ISSN 1070–1850)
    Includes index.
    ISBN 0–275–97026–4 (alk. paper)—ISBN 0–275–97539–8 (pbk. : alk. paper)
    1. Utopias.   2. Sociology.   3. Social problems.   I. Title: H.G. Wells on world revolution.   II. Title.   III. Series.
    HX811 .W45   2002
    321'.07—dc21   2001036692

British Library Cataloguing in Publication Data is available.

Copyright © 2002 by W. Warren Wagar

All rights reserved. No portion of this book may be reproduced, by any process or technique, without the express written consent of the publisher.

Library of Congress Catalog Card Number: 2001036692
ISBN: 0–275–97026–4
        0–275–97539–8 (pbk.)
ISSN: 1070–1850

First published in 2002

Praeger Publishers, 88 Post Road West, Westport, CT 06881
An imprint of Greenwood Publishing Group, Inc.
www.praeger.com

Printed in the United States of America

The paper used in this book complies with the Permanent Paper Standard issued by the National Information Standards Organization (Z39.48–1984).

10 9 8 7 6 5 4 3 2 1

Copyright Acknowledgment

Material from *The Open Conspiracy* by H.G. Wells copyright by the Literary Executors of the Estate of H.G. Wells. Reprinted with permission.

Contents

Critical Introduction

by W. Warren Wagar

Part One:

The First Futurist

1. The Book of the Century?

The small book you hold in your hands may be the most important book written in the 20th century. Whether it deserves such esteem depends on what happens in the 21st. If the human race against all odds manages to pull itself together and build a durable world civilization, *The Open Conspiracy* will be remembered as its Declaration of Interdependence, as the first clear statement of its destiny.

These are large claims, difficult to defend, and at first blush even preposterous. *The Open Conspiracy* was never a best seller, although its author published several books that were best sellers, from *The Time Machine* to *The Outline of History.* It sold only modestly, wielded no perceptible influence on the course of world events, attracted few enthusiasts, appears on nobody's list of the classic texts of modern thought or literature.[1] Until now it has long been out of print.

But the value of books is not always measured by sales or critical success or contemporary impact. The significance of a book may not be apparent until decades, even centuries have passed. One case in point is *The Time Machine* itself, H.G. Wells's first book (apart from two textbooks), which is surely far better known and appreciated than when it was published more than a hundred years ago. In its own era, *The Time Machine* was an amusing novelty. Today it belongs in the canon of great world literature. It has never been out of print.

The Open Conspiracy is of course a very different sort of book altogether. Such significance as it may have is neither belletristic nor philosophical nor sociological. Unlike *The Communist Manifesto,* which in some ways it resembles, it did not inspire the rise of a great worldwide political movement. At least not so far. And yet I repeat. *The Open Conspiracy* may be the most important book written in the 20th century. It contains a set of ideas and strategies of far greater urgency as humankind enters the next millennium than when it was first published in 1928. It offers a road map to the only kind of human future worth having, a future of universal peace, liberty, well-being, unity, and adventure, where all of us live in fraternity and sorority one with another, in a vast and ever-changing world-city that reaches from earth to the stars.

This is not to say that you will agree with everything you find in *The Open Conspiracy*. I certainly do not. If he were alive today, you can also be quite sure that H.G. Wells himself would not. His ideas about the desirable future evolved from year to year. He was often derided for his inconsistencies. In his last book, *Mind at the End of Its Tether* (1945), he even washed his hands of humanity and damned it to hell. I prefer to read *Mind at the End of Its Tether* as the tantrum of a sick and dying man. Still, living through the apocalypse of World War Two, which he had often foreseen in books of uncanny prescience, including *The World Set Free* (1914) and *The Shape of Things To Come* (1933), surely entitled the old prophet to a final fit of despair, his own version of "Eloi, Eloi, lama sabachthani." Had he recovered his health, I think he would have recanted and carried on with his usual courage. In any event, he would not have wished *The Open Conspiracy* to be seen as a sacred text, flawless and beyond reproach.

Nevertheless *The Open Conspiracy* is a book of enormous cogency. It offers guidelines for a world revolution, suggesting in some detail how humankind can effect the transition from the present-day global "system" of warlike sovereign states, megacorporate piracy, demographic overshoot, and spiritual anomie—so much like the world of Wells's own time—to a Cosmopolis of peace and plenty. Should we ever get there, it is a good bet that historians of ideas will hail *The Open Conspiracy* as its founding text.

2. H.G. Wells and Futures Studies

Herbert George Wells liked to refer to himself as a quite unexceptional man, who just happened to see things a bit more clearly and comprehensively than many of his contemporaries. He subtitled his *Experiment in Autobiography* (1934) *Discoveries and Conclusions of a Very Ordinary Brain*. In the second chapter of *The Open Conspiracy*, he begins by explaining that he is a "very ordinary, undistinguished person" with "a mediocre brain." (p. 54) The idea is that if someone of average intelligence—like Wells—can figure out what is happening to the world and how to remedy it, then so can Mr. Everyman and Miss Everywoman. The author is not in possession of occult wisdom. What he sees, anyone can see, with a modicum of effort. It is all just a matter of common sense.

Of course such modesty rings false, and the reader should not be taken in by it. Although H.G. Wells may not have had the astronomical intelligence quotient of a Bertrand Russell or an Albert Einstein, or the literary genius of a James Joyce, he was far from unexceptional. He was born into a barely middle-class family in Bromley, Kent, in 1866, the son of a small-time shopkeeper and a former lady's maid. From this stratum of Victorian society almost no one could hope to rise to a higher station in life, and almost no one did. Wells is practically the only literary man or woman of his generation with comparable origins. He was not working-class, but his father's little shop, together with some professional cricketing on the side, brought the Wells family only a meagre livelihood. Young Bert was apprenticed to various tradesmen in the early 1880s, the usual lot of a Victorian boy of his class, but he fought his way out of these situations, won a scholarship, went to London, studied for three years at the Normal School of Science in South Kensington, and passed his examinations for the bachelor's degree in science in 1889.

At first Wells saw himself as a science teacher and compiler of textbooks, roles he did fill satisfactorily for several years, but his teeming imagination soon propelled him into a wholly different career in free-lance writing. He began selling articles and stories in the early 1890s, scored a triumph with *The Time Machine*, and by the year 1900 had published no fewer than 16 books— two science textbooks, two collections of essays, four collections of short stories, and eight novels. The best remembered (besides *The Time Machine*) are his other early science-fiction novels, especially *The Island of Dr. Moreau* (1896), *The Invisible Man* (1897), and *The War of the Worlds* (1898).

Incredibly, he was able to maintain this pace for the remaining 46 years of his life, during which he produced another 104 books. These include such masterpieces of science fiction as *The First Men in the Moon* (1901), such genial comic novels as *Kipps* (1905) and *The History of Mr. Polly* (1910), such major novels of life and times as *Tono-Bungay* (1909) and *Mr. Britling Sees It Through* (1916), such magisterial compendia of knowledge as *The Outline of History* (1920) and *The Science of Life* (1931), such outstanding contributions to the literature of utopia as *A Modern Utopia* (1905) and *Men Like Gods* (1923), and his incomparable *Experiment in Autobiography* (1934), one of the finest autobiographies of this or any century.

But it would be a grave error to think of H.G. Wells simply as a popular and successful man of letters. Throughout his career, from *The Time Machine* to *Mind at the End of Its Tether*, the thread that ties all his prodigious writing together is an obsession with the future of humankind. I disagree with those many critics down through the years who have described Wells as an artist gone bad, a distinguished craftsman who could perhaps have attained literary immortality save for his tendency in middle and later years to spoil his art with the huckstering of half-baked ideas about this and that. When an artist becomes a propagandist, he loses his soul—so goes the oft-repeated lament.

Perhaps so. At least that was the doctrine of critics reared in the now faded modernist tradition. As a historian, not a literary critic, I am not overly concerned. In any event, I am clear about one thing. H.G. Wells was obsessed, fatally obsessed if you please, with the future of his species and with the question of how that species could dodge extinction and fulfill its destiny as a race of rational, creative, sociable beings. Should anyone, including a rather gifted writer, have to apologize for such an obsession? I think not.

And this obsession of Wells's most assuredly did not begin in his middle years. It was always there, right from the start. Among his earliest published essays were "The Man of the Year Million" (1893) and "The Extinction of Man" (1894). *The Time Machine* is a fantasy about what could happen to the human race hundreds of thousands of years from now if the class war between capital and labour continued without resolution to its ultimate dénouement. *When the Sleeper Wakes* (1899) imagined the class war in full rage in the year 2100. Two years later Wells published a set of substantial prophetic essays in *The Fortnightly Review*, issued in 1902 as a book under the title *Anticipations of the Reaction of Mechanical and Scientific Progress Upon Human Life and Thought*. In retrospect *Anticipations* may be seen as the cornerstone of modern futurism, the first serious and sustained attempt by a mind of Wells's calibre to foresee, in his own later phrase, "the shape of things to come." Some of its forecasts, especially having to do with transport, urban sprawl, warfare, and technology, have held up well. Others have not. But *Anticipations* was there, all 318 sturdy pages of it, long before Bertrand de Jouvenel, Edward Cornish, Herman Kahn, and other notables invented "futures studies" in the 1960s.[2]

Hard on the heels of *Anticipations* came another, shorter work, in which Wells not only practiced the art of futurism but called for its establishment as a field of scientific study. *The Discovery of the Future* (1902), originally a lecture at the Royal Institution, found Wells, as David C. Smith remarks, at his finest. "He used his scientific background and his command of the language to offer an opening into the future filled with light and promise."[3] At the same time, Wells peered confidently ahead to the day when science would "throw a searchlight of inference forward instead of backward, and...attain a knowledge of coming things as clear, as universally convincing, and infinitely more important to mankind than the clear vision of the past that geology has opened to us during the nineteenth century."[4] In a much later piece, a radio talk entitled "Wanted—Professors of Foresight!" (1932), he followed up his suggestion of 30 years previous with an appeal for the creation of "whole Faculties and Departments of Foresight doing all they can to anticipate and prepare for the consequences of this gathering together...what were once widely dispersed human relationships."[5]

Once established in people's minds as a prophet, Wells was able to devote a significant part of his writing from 1902 onward to essays, tracts, and novels explicitly centred on the human future. He had been a futurist from the beginning, but now he enjoyed a certain international standing as a specialist in matters futuristic. The success of *Anticipations* and *The Discovery of the Future* created a climate of public expectation that welcomed his every vatic utterance for the next 35 years. His final books and articles on the future, published in the late 1930s and early 1940s, fared less well, although his readers never entirely deserted him. The titles usually speak for themselves: to name just a few, *The Future in America* (1906), *New Worlds for Old* (1908), *The War That Will End War* (1914), *What Is Coming?* (1916), *A Year of Prophesying* (1924), *The Shape of Things To Come* (1933), the screenplay written by Wells himself for the 1936 Alexander Korda film *Things To Come, World Brain* (1938), and *The Outlook for Homo Sapiens* (1942). Nor should we omit *The Open Conspiracy* itself, which in its first edition bore the subtitle *Blue Prints for a World Revolution*.

All this, and much more, easily earns H.G. Wells the sobriquet of "founder of futures studies," as I have endeavoured to show in my book *The Next Three Futures*.[6] He was the first modern futurist. No one else approaches the contribution he made to this perilous and fragile science over a span of more than 50 years.

3. The World Commonweal

Between September, 1923, and September, 1924, Wells wrote a series of weekly articles for the McClure Newspaper Syndicate, articles that appeared in newspapers throughout the English-speaking world. All 54 pieces, and one other, were collected and published in 1924 as *A Year of Prophesying*. I should imagine that not more than a hundred people now alive have ever read it through. No doubt even fewer remember a word of it. Some of the pieces are not prophetic at all—for example a wickedly comic broadside against Winston Churchill and a ringing defence of the Spanish philosopher Miguel de Unamuno, exiled from Spain for criticizing the dictatorship of Miguel Primo de Rivera.

But just as many other pieces in the volume do centrally concern the future. Most of these focus on an institution that Wells never missed a chance to ridicule, the League of Nations. He had been active all through the Great War in lending his support to the idea of a League, but when it was finally put together by the victors at Versailles, he turned away from it in disgust, as just another gathering of diplomats representing the base interests of sovereign states: in short, a revolting parody of world government.

In the very first article, dated September 22, 1923, Wells contrasted the League as it existed with his own vision of the "Federation of Mankind." Wells's Federation would withdraw from states the right and power to make war; the League was nothing less than an obstacle to world federation, a way not to abolish diplomacy but merely to add one more piece to the diplomatic gameboard. In later articles, he grew more acerbic. The feeble efforts of the League were

> trivial, useless, and ridiculous. ... It is a blind alley for good intentions, it is a weedy dump for all the weaknesses of European liberalism. Its past is contemptible, and the briefer the future of its present constitution the better for mankind.

Exploring the future of the British Empire, he looked forward to the day when its trusteeship would end and all states and empires would be superseded

7

by an "inevitable world control," a "Federation of Peoples." But not the League of Nations. "The world is in urgent need of a real League of Nations and a real conference of peoples—this costume parade at Geneva is a mere mockery of its hopes."[7]

The article that I find most poignant in *A Year of Prophesying* is the piece Wells filed on December 29, 1923, "Cosmopolitan and International." He contrasted the words and their etymologies, and explained why he vastly preferred the first to the second, despite their connotations, one negative, the other positive, in current usage. Internationalism was symbolized, for Wells, by the League of Nations, with all its elaborate machinery to prop up the prevailing system of independent states. Under internationalism, every country had its own currency, its own trade walls, its own economy, its own form of government, holding its subjects prisoner. "The world is a patchwork of various sized internment camps called Independent Sovereign States, and we are each caught in our bit of the patchwork and cannot find a way of escape." By contrast, a "cosmopolitan" was simply a citizen of Cosmopolis, the City of the World, all the lands and all the cities of our pleasant earth. Nothing so angered the world-travelling Wells as having his books read and his underwear searched by customs officers. In Cosmopolis there would be no such appalling creatures.

> I am for world-control of production and of trade and transport, for a world coinage, and the confederation of mankind. I am for the super-State, and not for any League. Cosmopolis is my city, and I shall die cut off from it. When I die I shall have lived only a part of my possible life, a sort of life in a corner. And this is true of nearly all the rest of mankind alive at the present time.[8]

"Cosmopolis is my city." This could be the epigraph of *The Open Conspiracy* and perhaps of every book Wells ever wrote. One could disinter a thousand equally apt passages from his work to demonstrate that for H.G. Wells there could be no happy future for humankind unless it included the amalgamation of all nations, races, and climes under the banner of a single scientifically managed global polity. He called it many things—federation, confederation, world state, system of world controls, scientific world commonweal, cosmopolis, modern utopia, world directorate—but it was always much the same thing.

In *Anticipations,* for example, he wrote of the New Republic, a freemasonry of the competent and functional classes, who would in time build "the higher organism, the world-state of the coming years."[9] In his fictional alternative earth in *A Modern Utopia*, the Roman Empire had evolved into a modern world state without the long travail of an age of independent nations. Even in his novels of romance and high society, Wells managed to insinuate dreams of world integration. Stephen Stratton, the somewhat implausible hero of *The Passionate Friends* (1913), devoted his life to the construction of a worldwide publishing empire to help forge a sense of human solidarity. He and his American partner Gidding thought of themselves "as the citizens neither of the United States nor of England but of a state that had still to come into being, a World State, a great unity behind and embracing the ostensible political fabrics of to-day."[10] Months later, in the spring of 1914, Wells was out with yet another fictional scenario of the world state in being, *The World Set Free*, achieved this time in the aftermath of a grisly atomic war.

The ink had scarcely dried on copies of *The World Set Free* when a real war broke out; and not surprisingly, Wells hailed it as a historic opportunity to advance the cause of world integration. In a short book with the stirring title *The War That Will End War*, composed of newspaper articles all published during the first month of the Great War, Wells urged Great Britain and its allies to annihilate Prussian militarism, but only as the prelude to the calling of a postwar world conference. At this great conference, the map of Europe could be redrawn to minimize ethnic conflict. The conferees could then proceed to ban the private manufacture and trade of weapons of war and "set up a Peace League that will control the globe."[11]

Throughout the war, as noted above, Wells was an ardent supporter of the idea of a League of Nations. When the postwar world conference he had foreseen in 1914 actually took place, it shattered his hopes. But only briefly. The vision of a global polity or system of world controls reappeared time and again all through the next 25 years of his productive life. The last chapter of *The Outline of History*, entitled "The Next Stage in History," centred on the likely advent of what he variously termed "a federal world government" and a "modern world state." Achieving such a polity was the mission of the Open Conspiracy. It is the central theme of the last and longest chapter in his *Experiment in Autobiography*, entitled "The Idea of a Planned World." He described the emergence of a world state from the ashes of a second world war in *The Shape of Things To Come* and in the film based on that remarkable novel, *Things To Come*. He supplied the same scenario, essentially, in another novel published on the eve of the real World War Two, *The Holy Terror* (1939). And he continued his propaganda for Cosmopolis through most of the evil years of that all-too-real Armageddon, reviewing his plans and hopes one more time in *Phoenix: A Summary of the Inescapable Conditions of World Reorganization* (1942). As he had written in his autobiography several years before:

> I find...that this faith and service of constructive world revolution does hold together my mind and will in a prevailing unity, that it makes life continually worth living, transcends and minimizes all momentary and incidental frustrations and takes the sting out of the thought of death.[12]

In short, the service of a world revolution leading to the alliance of all humankind was, for Wells, no less than a religion. He said so, quite unambiguously, in the Preface to the first edition of *The Open Conspiracy*:

This book states as plainly and clearly as possible the essential ideas of my life, the perspective of my world. ... My other writings, with hardly an exception, explore, try over, illuminate, comment upon or flower out of the essential matter that I here attempt at last to strip bare to its foundations and state unmistakably. This is my religion. Here are my directive aims and the criteria of all I do.[13]

There is no compelling reason—Freudian or otherwise—not to take the man at his word.

Part Two:

What Are We To Do with Our Lives?

1. The Text

The Open Conspiracy that you will read here is not the first edition, although it contains most of the words of the first edition. The first was published by Victor Gollancz in Britain and by Doubleday in the United States, and contained a Preface, 17 numbered chapters, and a concluding "Note on the Margin of These Blue Prints." Two years later, in 1930, Leonard and Virginia Woolf published a revised second edition at the Hogarth Press, under the title *The Open Conspiracy: A Second Version of This Faith of a Modern Man Made More Explicit and Plain.* Then, in 1931, Wells tried his hand again, retitling the book *What Are We To Do with Our Lives?* The Preface and the "Note on the Margin of These Blue Prints" had now disappeared and the 17 original chapters had grown to 19, the first four new, with the fifth incorporating material from the first three in the original edition. Here and there through the 15 chapters that remained essentially the same in both editions, Wells added a few passages or omitted others, but *What Are We To Do with Our Lives?* was less a rewriting of *The Open Conspiracy* than a modestly expanded version of the same book, with a new title. *What Are We To Do with Our Lives?* was also reprinted in 1935 and again in 1938 by Watts of London as the 55th volume in its popular series *The Thinker's Library.*

It is curious to note, however, that in 1933 Waterlow and Sons published the 1931 edition of *What Are We To Do with Our Lives?* under its original title, *The Open Conspiracy.* Two other Wells books, *First and Last Things* (1908) and *Russia in the Shadows* (1920), were also reprinted in this rather odd omnibus volume. Stuffing these three mismatched books together may not have made much sense, but in one respect Waterlow and Sons had probably got it right: although *What Are We To Do with Our Lives?* was a better book than its first edition, *The Open Conspiracy* had the better title.

Wells also took the opportunity in this little-known 1933 reprint to make a few minor alterations in the 1931 text. All of these alterations were clearly improvements, but were not incorporated into the 1935 edition published by *The Thinker's Library.* In the edition you now have before you, we have therefore reprinted the 1933 text, including its restoration of the 1928 title. The

1931 title, *What Are We To Do with Our Lives?*, suggests a self-improvement book by some oily New Age guru intent on expanding our consciousness or teaching us the fulfilling joys of charitable good works (such as sending a large bank cheque to his or her Fellowship). *The Open Conspiracy* is a uniquely Wellsian call to world revolution on behalf of Cosmopolis.

2. The World Crisis and Modern Religion

The best part about the 1931-35 editions of *The Open Conspiracy*—as opposed to the original edition—is perhaps their first chapter, "The Present Crisis in Human Affairs." Read it carefully. It is vintage Wells, written when the real world was at peace, but on the brink of a spasm of wars, from China, Ethiopia, and Spain, to the ultimate holocaust of World War Two. Wells notes three great abolitions that have changed the whole agenda of humankind—the abolition of distance, the abolition of shortage of supply, and the abolition of the shortness of life, all made possible by science and technology, but enjoyed, as yet, by only a privileged minority of our species. The reason for this deplorable state of affairs was not far to seek. Our institutions had not kept pace with our powers. The world was run by politicians (always a favourite target of Wells's) in the service of a system of sovereign states that by its nature bred war and injustice.

What to do? Join the Open Conspiracy. This is Wells's phrase for a loose-knit global movement of ideas and actions aimed at the replacement of the system of sovereign states with another system altogether, which, in 1931, he found foreshadowed in the first Soviet Five-Year Plan, a deliberate and heroic effort to reconstruct a whole vast society spanning two continents. Wells was temperamentally hostile to Marxism and Soviet autocracy, but his imagination was captured by this strenuous effort to convert Russia into a modern indus-trialized state. The task undertaken by Stalin's Bolsheviks on a regional scale might foretell what all humankind under the leadership of the advanced peoples of the Atlantic world could achieve on a world scale, if their functional elites—men of business, science, technology, and industry—banded together in an open, above-ground, and candid struggle to transcend the now woefully obsolete nation-state system.

The struggle would begin, as Wells had always insisted, with an intellectu-al renaissance. We must, he contended, "clear and clean up our minds." Modern science and social science had furnished our species with the knowl-edge it needed to convert earth into a veritable paradise, but most of us were badly educated and grievously ignorant, unprepared mentally to enter the dawning era of peace, abundance, and cosmopolitanism. With help from experts, Wells himself had written three books that together supplied much of this essential knowledge (*The Outline of History*; *The Science of Life*; *The Work, Wealth and Happiness of Mankind*). But wherever the would-be world citizen obtained a basic understanding of earth and its people, he or she could not expect to join the struggle to build Cosmopolis without a well-stocked and up-to-date brain. The remedy was a revolution in education, to ensure that every new citizen possessed a comprehensive, scientific world-view. Failing this, there could be no hope for the kind of fundamental reconstruction Wells envisaged. As he had proclaimed in *The Outline of History* (and for some odd reason this remains one of his best remembered lines), "Human history becomes more and more a race between education and catastrophe."[14]

The fifth and sixth chapters of *The Open Conspiracy*, in the edition here reprinted, are devoted to something that Wells prized even above knowledge. Like his great predecessor in global utopography, Auguste Comte, who insisted in *The System of Positive Polity* (1851-1854) that beyond a comprehensive knowledge of modern science the new world order required a "Religion of Humanity," Wells appreciated the need for a spiritual dimension in life. As we saw above, the idea of the Open Conspiracy was his religion—not his point of view, or his ideology, or his political philosophy, but his religion. For Wells religion meant devotion and commitment to something greater than oneself. Traditional religion found that greater something in supernatural personages, but for the modern man and woman, disabused by science of such ancient fantasies, the only object worthy of devotion was humankind itself, humankind as a species evolving and lifting itself millennium by millennium to ever greater realization of its possibilities. Comte had called it "the Great Being of Humanity," but for Wells it was more like the "Great Becoming." People who consecrated their lives to its service would be able to accomplish what the possession of mere knowledge alone could never motivate them to do. They would be warriors for the coming world civilization, never resting until it was achieved; and, of course, not even then, for with the end of the old history, a new history, a finer and higher history than anything known hitherto, would begin.

3. Management, Not Government

Having set forth the nature of the 20th-century global crisis and introduced the idea of an Open Conspiracy of scientifically educated men and women devoted to the service of humanity, Wells proceeded in his seventh and eighth chapters to spell out in some detail what kind of new world order his Conspirators would strive to create. The term he used here is "a scientific world commonweal." Although he had spoken in earlier writings of a world "federation" or even "confederation," his life-long distrust of politicians and electoral democracy did not allow him to believe with any sort of real conviction in the model of government furnished by states such as Great Britain, France, or the United States. In *The Open Conspiracy* he did not even try. He made it quite clear that what he had in mind was less a world state or world

13

government than a system of global management of human affairs by "suitably equipped groups of the most interested, intelligent, and devoted people...subjected to a free, open, watchful criticism" (p. 71 below). The Open Conspiracy, as it evolved, would transform itself into a world directorate charged with running humanity's public affairs in the most efficient way possible. In the jargon of political science, Wells was not so much a federalist as a "functionalist," an advocate of the gradual take-over of the world by qualified experts in science, technology, and public administration.

This may sound either hopelessly naive or profoundly sinister, but it was always Wells's vision of the world polity whenever he came down from his eloquent rhetorical high road and forced himself to cope with everyday details. As he concedes in the middle of his seventh chapter,

> Some method of decision there must certainly be and a definite administrative machinery. But it may turn out to be a much slighter, less elaborate organization than a consideration of existing methods might lead us to imagine. It may never become one single interlocking administrative system. We may have systems of world control rather than a single world state. (p. 72, below)

Wells was not speaking, however, of innocuous agencies like those of the League of Nations or of the United Nations today. He defined the Open Conspiracy on this same page as a "world movement for the supersession or enlargement or fusion of existing political, economic, and social institutions." The British and French parliaments and cabinets, the United States Congress and presidency, the Weimar Reichstag, and so forth would no longer go about their business just as they pleased and just as they had always done. They would have been replaced or incorporated into higher bodies. No nation would remain sovereign or independent. The planet would be managed by the Open Conspiracy in its epiphany as a world directorate.

The eighth chapter, "Broad Characteristics of a Scientific World Commonweal," is in some ways the meatiest in the book and deserves a close reading. After a brief discussion of the need for the Open Conspiracy to remain open and above-ground, Wells fired his usual volley of attacks on Marxism and the notion of class warfare. Both classical and Marxist economic theory must be scrapped, he argued, and replaced by a truly scientific economics, embodying the latest insights of industrial psychology and scientific management. There was no necessary antagonism between employers and employees, if both would only open their minds to the possibilities of mutual effort for the common weal (as in the conclusion of the great Fritz Lang film *Metropolis* [1926], in concept strongly reminiscent of Wells's 1899 science-fiction novel *When the Sleeper Wakes*).

Nevertheless, Wells did not entirely abandon his youthful faith in socialism. He had no further use for notions of inevitable class struggle, fantasized in *The Time Machine*, but he also continued to believe that in a scientific world state much of the economy would necessarily be transferred from private to public hands. In this eighth chapter he called for public ownership of land and the high seas, of wildlife, and of the production and distribution of all "staple products" as well as transport. A central world authority would also set up a global monetary and financial system. Wells did not define the sphere remaining to private enterprise, but by implication it would be restricted to the production of goods and services that could be described as luxuries or items of discretionary consumption, such as fine wines or recordings of music or ocean cruises. Much depends on how one chooses to construe the adjective "staple." What is a staple in the 1990s might not have been a staple in the 1920s, and what is a staple in a contemporary Chelsea flat may not be a staple in a contemporary Bangladeshi village.

The ninth chapter of *The Open Conspiracy* makes the brief but vital point that once the world civilization was in place, it would not stand still. Human life is an eternal becoming. The tenth chapter again challenges Marxism, in particular its Soviet incarnation, and at the same time reiterates Wells's lack of faith in any sort of revolution from below, captained by the working class. The Open Conspiracy would be formed and led by an elite of intelligent and creative recruits from all classes, and in particular by the "functional" sort of people, the people who actually manage the world's work, as opposed to the idlers at the top and the inert masses at the bottom. Wells admitted that many of these functional folk might be motivated only by greed and self-interest, but in every class one found a stratum of creative people, who worked for higher ends. These creative types, the salt of Wells's earth, would flock to the Open Conspiracy and lead it to victory.

4. Resistances

Or perhaps not. Victory was not assured unless all the many and mighty opposing forces in the modern world could be neutralized. The next three chapters, the eleventh through the thirteenth, consider who and what would resist the coming of the scientific world commonweal. In the advanced nations, the countries of what Wells termed the "Atlantic civilizations," the Open Conspiracy would find its greatest opportunities but also some of its most implacable foes.

Foremost among these oppositional forces was the blind loyalty to existing states and governments carefully nurtured by the ruling classes of every state—politicians, diplomats, civil service bureaucrats, generals, and the like. Since the Open Conspiracy schemed to supersede the existing governments, they would not be readily tolerant of it. They might consider it treasonous. Of course every good Open Conspirator would surely return the favour. "Loyalty to 'king and country' passes into plain treason to mankind" (p. 90, below). Nevertheless, it would be no simple matter for Open Conspirators to defend themselves against the armed might of the prevailing order.

In this connection, let it be noted that in his previous chapter, in discussing the membership of the Open Conspiracy, Wells had already made quite obvious his willingness to wage bloody war, if necessary, against that prevailing order. He was no pacifist. "Since there are armies prepared to act coercively in the world to-day, it is necessary that the Open Conspiracy should develop within itself the competence to resist military coercion and combat and destroy armies that stand in the way of its emergence" (p. 86, below; cf. p. 132, below). Obviously whole armies could not be destroyed without a countervailing military force of one's own. Wells furnished few details but on this point there can be no doubt.

At any rate, the governments and armies of the old regimes would be a major obstacle to the mission of the Open Conspiracy. By the same token, the Open Conspiracy would find itself under attack from reactionary elements in religious and educational institutions, by long tradition adjuncts of the political establishment. Churches and schools could sometimes be subverted, and no doubt more easily than governments, but the task would be onerous.

Wells was more hopeful of the chances of the Open Conspiracy in its dealings with the business community. The natural interest of businessmen in free global trade should, he thought, incline them to join rather than oppose the Open Conspiracy. But many of their number would hold back, preferring the privileges and honors dangled under their noses by the bosses of the national state to the more austere rewards of good world citizenship.

What, then, of resistances in the world beyond the Atlantic civilizations? What of the less industrialized peoples, some of them still in a state of savagery or at least barbarism, and the greater number [i.e., in 1931] under Western colonial administration? The finer minds in Asia and Africa might actually welcome the Open Conspiracy, seeing it as a way to escape "the sinking vessel of their antiquated order" (p. 100, below) and the chafing rule of European imperial masters at one and the same time. Unfortunately, more traditionally-minded Asians and Africans would view the Open Conspiracy as just a new-fangled scheme by Europeans and Americans to perpetuate their envelopment of the less industrialized world. As for Russia, Wells saw a glimmer of hope that the Bolshevik elite now ruling this vast nation would ultimately come on board the Open Conspiracy, but he had none at all for the great mass of the Russian peasantry, or for that matter the Chinese. He saw in their ranks "a vastly wider ignorance and a vastly more formidable animalism" than anything Open Conspirators would confront in the Western world (p. 102, below).

So, on balance, the Open Conspiracy would encounter much more serious resistance outside Europe and the Americas than inside; and in any event, only in the Atlantic nations (and perhaps in Westernized Japan) were there enough scientifically educated people and enough freedom of discussion and criticism to launch the Open Conspiracy and sustain it in its early decades.

Yet even here, in the relatively enlightened Atlantic world, and even in its most enlightened men and women, the Conspiracy would experience opposition. Wells's thirteenth chapter makes the useful point that we have to worry not only about what others may do but also about the darker or less creative elements in our own natures: the "everydayism" that seduces us from our higher tasks, the problem of sustaining religious commitment without binding rituals, the tugs of old and obsolescent loyalties, the streaks of destructiveness, jealousy, and cruelty found in all of us, no matter how bright or vigorous or progressive we may think ourselves to be. "You have not yet completed your escape to the Open Conspiracy from the cities of the plain," Wells sternly warned, "while it is still possible for you to take a single backward glance" (p. 109, below).

In another, earlier age, might Wells have been a Calvinist divine, or the author of *Pilgrim's Progress?* The question is worth pondering.

5. Strategies and Tactics

The remaining chapters of *The Open Conspiracy* address primarily the issue of how to get from now to then—in short, strategies and tactics. The Open Conspiracy would begin, thought Wells, as a movement of discussion, involving many groups of various sizes linked only by a common pledge to regard all loyalties to existing governments as provisional, to work for global population control, and to resist national preparations for war. In the context of the late 1920s and early 1930s, he viewed a worldwide campaign to refuse service in any future wars as the best immediate project to bring right-minded people together. By this point in European history, moral revulsion against the Great War was reaching its apogee, ten years and more after the Armistice. It was the time when Erich Maria Remarque published his powerful anti-war novel *All Quiet on the Western Front* (1929), and when pacifism was actively promoted as a populist antidote to militarism, above all in Britain. The days of the Peace Pledge Union in Britain were not far off.

Again, however, Wells was no doctrinaire pacifist. Open Conspirators were to pledge non-participation in future wars engineered by the national states, but this ought not to preclude, he insisted, military training and action "on behalf of the world commonweal for the suppression of nationalist brigandage" (p. 112, below). Once again he had bravely broached the prospect of Open Conspiracy militias doing battle with ignorant national armies, but he had omitted all the pertinent details. It is hard to imagine how such militias could have been raised given his further assertion that the Open Conspiracy must not begin as—and should not ever become—a single organization with a single chain of command. Rather it would serve as the ideological umbrella for innumerable smaller groups each acting more or less independently, linked by common goals and ideas, but without a hierarchy. Wells offered the Soviet Communist Party and the Roman Catholic Church as models of what the

Open Conspiracy should *not* become, at any cost.

Nevertheless, anyone claiming to be an Open Conspirator would need to swear by seven "broad principles" enumerated at the close of the fourteenth chapter, including commitment to the formation of a "world directorate" competent to end warfare, transfer ownership of transport and staple production to itself, control population growth and disease, and establish a global minimum standard of freedom and welfare. Obviously no invertebrate assortment of overlapping organizations could be expected to manage the affairs of a whole planet. At some point the Open Conspiracy would have to come together to constitute the world directorate, and there could not be more than one of these. At least so I read Wells's intentions, his understandable distrust of hierarchy notwithstanding.

The fifteenth, sixteenth, and seventeenth chapters of *The Open Conspiracy* discuss the early constructive work of Open Conspirators and the likelihood of their finding allies in already existing progressive movements. Wells invited collaboration with many *ad hoc* initiatives in the world of the early 1930s, from associations of businessmen and the campaign for birth control (Margaret Sanger was for a time one of his lovers) to societies for alternative schooling and political movements aimed at replacing local and regional bodies with a system of world controls. The sixteenth chapter closes with a parable that neatly sums up the totalism implicit in Wells's vision. I shall leave it to your reading, but it reduces, in effect, to the policy of the "whole hog." The only way to make a meaningful difference in today's world, said Wells, was to slay the old order in its entirety, feet, snout, tail, and torso. The old Fabian strategy of gradualism and permeation would not suffice.

In the eighteenth chapter, Wells looked somewhat further into the future, to the time when the Open Conspiracy would be in position to take power. What hazards would it face? What risks would it run? How should Conspirators act if their activities were blocked by armed authorities? Fight, flee, or fiddle? Wells's answer was plain. Wherever the Open Conspiracy was forcibly prevented from doing its work of persuasion and illumination, "it must fight" (p. 131, below). In the Atlantic world, Wells guessed that violence would not be necessary. Countries like Britain, France, and "republican Germany" (Weimar Germany, not Hitler's Third Reich, which did not yet exist in 1931[15]) would no doubt tolerate their Conspirators, and could be won over with only minor struggles. Conspirators would be unlikely to face jail sentences, let alone armed attack. Yet if force were used to suppress them, "the Open Conspiracy, to the best of its ability and the full extent of its resources, must become a fighting force and organize itself upon resistant lines." Nonresistance was "no part of the programme of the Open Conspiracy" (p. 132, below).

It was much likelier, however, that parts of the non-Western world would oppose the Conspiracy with force. The time might come when the Atlantic communities, under the banner of the Open Conspiracy, would be required to disarm and pacify these backward regions. Wells had no use for the "pedantry" of do-good internationalists who insisted on the right of every nation to conduct its own affairs, no matter how nefarious. It might well be necessary to impose peace and freedom by force. If he were alive today, it is arguable that Wells would have applauded the various efforts of the United States, NATO, and the United Nations in the 1990s to "pacify" Panama, Iraq, Somalia, Bosnia, and the like. He would not have mistaken any of these intervening powers for the Open Conspiracy, I am sure, but he might have found merit in their interventions nonetheless, as a crude anticipation of the new world order of his prophetic vision.

Then, as if awakening from a pleasant dream, Wells conceded in the last three paragraphs of this eighteenth chapter that his confidence in the good will and peaceful intentions of the Atlantic communities could be misplaced. Many vested interests would perhaps feel threatened and raise up a storm of resistance greater than anything he had imagined. Even the present-day (1931) peace among the Atlantic nations might break down at any time, leading to a second Great War vastly more destructive than the first. Open Conspirators might be called upon to die for their cause. "The establishment of the world community will surely exact a price—and who can tell what that price may be?—in toil, suffering, and blood" (p. 134, below). Nine years later, immediately after becoming Prime Minister in the midst of a second Great War that would bear out all of Wells's fears, his old sparring partner Winston Churchill used some of the same words in addressing the House of Commons.

6. A Critical Assessment: Negative

Wells gave the impression in this book that the project of an Open Conspiracy leading to a world commonweal was something freshly hatched. To be sure, *The Open Conspiracy* was up till then his most elaborate attempt in a work of non-fiction to suggest what needed doing to rescue humanity from its own inertia and wanton destructiveness.[16] But the strategies themselves—just like his obsession with the future and his vision of the world commonweal—can be traced back to some of his earliest writings, as I have done at length in my *H.G. Wells and the World State*.[17]

I shall not repeat all that here, but the most salient landmarks in the evolution of the idea of an Open Conspiracy are the New Republican movement discussed in *Anticipations*, the Order of the Samurai in *A Modern Utopia*, the cult of the world state in The Salvaging of Civilization (1921), and, most explicitly, the Open Conspiracy of global business interests described in abundant detail in Wells's longest novel, *The World of William Clissold* (1926). This novel marks Wells's first formal use of the phrase "open conspiracy," but there are incidental references to an open conspiracy in several of Wells's earlier books, going back as far as 1914.[18] In the 1930s and 1940s, Wells

19

invented still more open conspiracies, under new names: the Modern State Society in *The Shape of Things To Come*, the Party of the Common Man in *The Holy Terror*, and the World Revolutionary Movement in *Phoenix*.

What can be said about these strategies for world reconstruction, and in particular about the plans laid before his fellow men and women by H.G. Wells in *The Open Conspiracy*? Remarkably little attention has been paid to them by Wells scholars—mostly literary critics and biographers, far more interested in the fiction or the man or both than in his religion of the world state. Most of them have lacked any sort of core belief in the necessity either of such a religion or of such a solution to the manifold problems of 20th-century civilization.

This is not the case with the present writer. I have spent all of my adult life as a votary of Wells's religion, and I am a fervent believer in the imperative need for a social-democratic unitary world state. *The Open Conspiracy* is the most compelling book I have ever read. It has helped to shape all my thinking over the past 50 years since I first came upon it. So have many of Wells's other books, but *The Open Conspiracy* first and foremost.[19]

Such a *confessio fidei* on my part may render me ineligible in your eyes to assess this text critically. That would be perfectly understandable. All the same, I am no slavish follower of Wells's thought, any more than he was himself, and my generation is thrice removed from his. I was only a boy of 14 when he died; my life history has been radically different and I have been exposed to many influences unavailable to him during his lifetime. I do not view Wells as a "very ordinary" man. He was, far from that, quite extraordinary. But I do not revere him. It is possible that had we been contemporaries we would not have cared for each other at all. The Wells of the biographies, at least, is not the sort of human being I would want as a friend. I do not condemn him for what is nowadays smarmily referred to as his "life-style," but our temperaments would very likely not have meshed.

Much more to the point, I strongly dissent from some of the most important elements of Wells's world-revolutionary credo. It is time now to explain how and why I sometimes dissent, and also to explain how and why I often agree fully with the ideas expressed in this book, even though they were set down years before I was born and belong to a moment of world history that I did not personally experience.

I find at least seven considerable problems with the scheme for global reconstruction defended in *The Open Conspiracy*, and I shall address them in reverse order of their seriousness. The first—and least critical—is Wells's call in Chapter 14 for a campaign of citizen refusal to take part in future patriotic wars. This proposal came from the same man who in 1914 wrote, "Every sword that is drawn against Germany now is a sword drawn for peace"[20]. It came from the same man who supported with grim enthusiasm the still greater war to smash fascism that began in 1939. Admittedly, the idea of using war resistance to inaugurate the Open Conspiracy, given the very different state of world politics in the late 1920s and early 1930s, was less problematic than it would have been at almost any other time during Wells's long life. But Wells was no pacifist, as we have seen. Nor was he given to fantasies about spontaneous popular uprisings. He knew how the world worked, as well as anybody. He knew that masses of people could not be persuaded to risk their lives in higher causes without extensive re-education. He also knew that the flaws in the world order of his time were not superficial but deeply structural, irremediable by piecemeal measures. In retrospect his idea of war resistance in *The Open Conspiracy* seems merely opportunistic, even un-Wellsian.

A second problem that I have with *The Open Conspiracy* is its largely dismissive attitude towards Asia, Africa, and the rest of the non-Western world. The prophet was profoundly Eurocentric in his world-outlook, although never anti-American. He generally referred to the United States as a full partner with Western Europe in the mission of rebuilding civilization. But he entertained little hope in at least the short term for the non-Western majority of humankind. Their cultures were "effete," "decadent," and "antiquated," their teeming masses ignorant. On the whole, it may even have been a blessing in disguise that advanced and incidentally white empire-builders and colonists came among them and took them under their tutelage. It would be a major task of the Open Conspiracy to carry this process of Westernization to its logical finale, the creation of a modern scientific (hence Western) world commonweal that would benevolently, like a good father, lead these less fortunate souls into the new world order. In a way, this was exactly what the Bolsheviks were already trying to accomplish throughout the vast stretches of their polyglot and only half-civilized Eurasian empire. The Open Conspiracy would play such a role on a global scale.

Now it is perfectly true that Wells wrote *The Open Conspiracy* at a time when most liberal Western intellectuals shared the assumption of most conservative thinkers that white Western civilization was vastly superior to anything found in the non-Western world and that it was the white man's burden to carry the light of his higher culture into these darker, more distressed, and largely senescent lands. Wells was not quite a racist; he rejected doctrines of the inherent inferiority of the non-white races; but he could hardly believe in the liberating power of modern science and modern socialism and preach his secular religion of world integration (all thought-systems, he would have said, of strictly Western provenance) and, in the same breath, argue that the West had not overtaken and surpassed the East. Of course the West was leading the way to Cosmopolis. Therefore the only chance that non-Western peoples had of getting there, too, was to follow in the footsteps of their Western trailblazers. So spoke Wells.

My concern with this line of thinking is not so much its blatant Eurocentrism as its failure to give due weight to the revolutionary potential of these same non-Western peoples. To be sure, Asians, Africans, and Indo-Latins needed, and still need, to learn much from the West. It is no good to scorn

Christianity or Judaism as crumbling skeletal relics of a pre-scientific past, on the one hand, and privilege Islam, Hinduism, Buddhism, or Rastafarianism on the other. Science, socialism, and secularism all have deep roots (or parallel growths can be traced) in non-Western intellectual traditions, but no one can doubt that in the last few centuries they have fared best and forged farthest in Western countries. Well and good.

The fact remains that Asians, Africans, and Indo-Latins have been the principal historic victims of Western imperialism and capitalism. The fact remains that Western affluence is, to a considerable extent, predicated on Eastern and Southern poverty, and specifically on the poverty of those "teeming masses" Wells so casually wrote off. Of course this is even truer today than it was in Wells's lifetime. All the same, I think it was in 1928 or 1931 and is still today a grave error to discount the potential for world-revolutionary action of the non-Western peoples. They have more reason, more incentive to want the world state than their Western counterparts. They are quick studies. What they need to learn from the West they can learn, and in numberless instances have already learned. The Open Conspiracy could begin in China or India or Brazil as readily as in France or the United States.

A third problem I have with *The Open Conspiracy* is the mirror image of the second. Just as Wells may have underestimated the revolutionary potential of the Asian, African, and Indo-Latin peoples, so I would argue that he overestimated the good will and progressive intent of the European and North American peoples. The role he assigned to the "Atlantic" nations in the eighteenth chapter is, as he himself all but admitted, more wishful thinking than sound analysis. Ironically, those same gloriously up-to-date Atlantic nations were only eight years away from starting to blow one another to smithereens in World War Two when the 1931 edition of *The Open Conspiracy* appeared.

Today conditions in the Atlantic world for revolutionary initiatives may seem more propitious at first glance. We have a "republican Germany" once again and totalitarianism of the Mussolini, Hitler, and Stalin style is out of fashion altogether. The Western European nations have crafted an economic community that could serve as the nucleus for a future United States of Europe. But we are not one centimetre closer to cosmopolis. Western neo-imperialism flourishes worldwide, using local governments as its stooges, a far less costly arrangement than the old colonial administrations. All but a handful of the top 500 multinational corporations are based in these same Atlantic countries and in what Wells called in his twelfth chapter "Westernized" Japan. It is clearly in the vested interests of the elites of the Atlantic and Pacific Rim nations to crush with all their energy any initiative to build a socialist world order, and as of now they have the guns and the dollars to make resistance to their sway both foolhardy and futile.

We come now to the fourth problem, which is perhaps another facet of Wells's overestimation of the West. In *The Open Conspiracy* and in virtually all his writing, Wells's ingenuous late Victorian faith in the natural and social sciences is no longer cogent, and was already somewhat dated in the 1920s. My exposure since the early 1950s, first to Anglo-Austrian logical positivism, then to French existentialism, then to the relativistic historicism of Wilhelm Dilthey and Carl Becker, and finally to poststructuralist deconstruction, has left me quite incapable of seeing "science" as anything better than a set of alternative ways of playing elegant intellectual games with the world of sensory phenomena. Science gives us a number of alternative ways of sorting out these phenomena, and some of these ways powerfully enhance our ability to manipulate phenomena to our advantage, but science does not give us anything like objective truth.

To be fair, Wells rarely allowed himself to be dazzled by scientists. In our text he saw them as "less like a host of guiding angels than like a swarm of marvellous bees—endowed with stings" (p. 116, below). Yet science itself he did trust to provide humankind with an almost angelic sense of direction. People who knew their science, who knew the "right" way to do things, because science told them what it was, should simply be given the opportunity to go ahead and do them. This was always his faith, and I do not share it for a moment. Subjectivity, not to mention class and personal interest, and the prison bars of language, lie at the heart of all the pronouncements of science, from astrophysics to social psychology, and the best we can hope for in this imperfect universe is now and then to achieve a provisional consensus of the cognoscenti on what may or may not be true—for now. As I wrote long ago in *The City of Man*, our last resort may be "the will to agree."[21]

This brings us to my fifth problem, Wells's paradoxical preference for a decentralized and acephalous revolutionary movement, as you will find it clearly expressed in the tenth and fourteenth chapters. I say paradoxical because I cannot square this preference with his ultimate goal, the building of a network of global controls that would regulate the behaviour of the world's billions of inhabitants, and would be able to do so only after disempowering the sovereign state system and private capital, even matching their armed might with its own if need be. It is easy enough to understand why Wells had little use for rigid hierarchies and chains of command—he was personally no sort of politician or demagogue, and he put his faith in science to show the way.

But I cannot reconcile his vision of how the Open Conspiracy would be structured—or rather, not structured—and the tremendous tasks he assigned it to undertake. Nor, for that matter, can I reconcile his vision of the Open Conspiracy as a multiplicity of mostly uncoordinated movements with the other versions of the Open Conspiracy that appear in his fiction. The Order of the Samurai in *A Modern Utopia*, the Modern State Society and Air Dictatorship of *The Shape of Things To Come*, and Rud Whitlow's Party of the Common Man in *The Holy Terror* were unified and hierarchical organizations designed to run the world. On occasion, Wells may have been a more practical and realistic thinker in his novels than in his tracts, and I suspect that indeed he was.[22]

There was also a very stubborn, close to pig-headed streak of anti-Marxism in Wells that went far towards diluting his socialism and diverting it from its proper course. This anti-Marxism runs all through his work, and bubbles up alarmingly from time to time in the pages of *The Open Conspiracy*. Consider only the relevant passages in chapters 8, 10, 11, and 12. I would call this my sixth major problem with the text at hand, and since I am taking these seven objections in reverse order of seriousness, the sixth is almost the most serious.

Now it should go without saying that I do not quarrel with Wells's indictment of the dogmatic rigidity of much of what passed for Marxism in his time, above all in its Leninist-Stalinist manifestation. But even in the 1920s there were many Marxisms, and through the rest of the century many more appeared, so that today the best informed historians of political thought have long since lost count. What I find so obtuse about Wells's anti-Marxism is his refusal to grasp the structural dynamics of multinational capitalism and the worldwide class struggle it has engendered. He could have learned all this from Marx and Engels, and from some of their most vigorous successors and debtors, but he *would* not. He would not learn out of sheer annoyance with the more parrot-like elements of Marxist jargon, a certain residual petty bourgeois snobbery, and a typically Anglophone aversion to high theory. So he succumbed in *The Open Conspiracy* and elsewhere (especially in *The World of William Clissold*) to the delusion that because corporate leaders had much to gain from a global market safeguarded by a new world order, many of them would make splendid recruits to the Open Conspiracy. Meanwhile he abhorred the Marxist notion of implacable class warfare, if it meant hitching the wagon of the Open Conspiracy to the brawny bodies of largely mindless proletarians.

Wells was too perceptive a futurist to caricature Marxism in this fashion. As he noted in his eleventh chapter, "Labour is in revolt because as a matter of fact it is, in the ancient and exact sense of the word, ceasing to be labour at all" (p. 97, below). This is a typically far-sighted Wellsian observation. The Western working class in his time, and much more in ours, was indeed becoming a class of well educated, skilled, and politically alert people of many trades and professions, from machinists to physicians, from electrical engineers to university dons. Yet Wells apparently had difficulty seeing that all those who work for a living, no matter what the colour of their collars, all those who depend on wages and salaries and commissions and fees for all or most of their livelihood, are indeed members of the working class, fair game for exploitation in varying degrees by their capitalist bosses. Such bosses—principal stockholders and their chief executives—have no choice but to exploit workers and co-opt politicians, if they are to compete successfully, stay in business, and make a fat profit. It is their job.

But why stop there? What about the hundreds of millions of educable workers in the non-Western nations fit for most of the global economy's hard labour and willing to toil for a meagre fraction of the already modest price of the Western working class? The workers and peasants of these nations were furnishing the West with a goodly percentage of its foodstuffs, raw materials, and manufactured goods even in Wells's time. He knew that percentage could only rise as the century wore on.

It follows that the essential Marxian insights into the relentless drive for growth and profit as the engine of capitalism, the trend to monopoly or oligopoly ownership of the means of production, and the inevitability of the global exploitation of labour, remain as plausible in our century as they were in Marx's. How much predictive value they have for the 21st century, we shall soon find out.

But my point is that the Open Conspiracy, as a socialist world movement aiming at the transfer of the private ownership of the greater part of capital to public authorities, would necessarily regard multinational and megacorporate capital as a mortal enemy, and would be deeply engaged in the politics of class struggle. In short, the Open Conspiracy would be in the business of constructing a worldwide league of workers and could expect short shrift from the rank and file of principal stockholders everywhere. But Wells did not choose to cast his Conspiracy in such a light. Instead, he echoed the stale liberal cant and militant fascist ballyhoo of his time, with their claims (in very different tones) that all of us, from tycoons to turnip-diggers, belonged to one great society. *Ein Volk, Ein Reich*, and so forth.

We approach now the seventh and gravest of my problems with *The Open Conspiracy*. I do not mean to imply by the last sentence of the last paragraph that H.G. Wells was a closet Nazi. Of course not.[23] All the same, he harboured a deep, intractable, and, in the final analysis, dangerous antipathy to the whole idea of democracy, of government by the people. His ardent faith in science, his distrust of the labouring poor, and his populist contempt for politicians conspired to rob him of any sympathy or patience with the toilsome ways of democratic politics.[24] But without reading another word of Wells beyond the text that follows, you can easily take my point. Almost every page of *The Open Conspiracy* vibrates with disdain for democracy.

For example, consider this remark: "The favourite platitude of the politician, excusing himself for the futilities of his business, is that 'moral progress has not kept pace with material advance'" (p. 51, below). An innocent wisecrack? Not in context. We are told that politicians push platitudes and that their business is futile. Later, Wells advises us that "kings, presidents, and so forth, are really not directive heads. They are merely the figure heads." Rulers and dictators were in fact "dummies" (p. 71, below). But who were the ventriloquists? Wells's explanation was deliberately vague. His was surely not the Marxist explanation that rulers and dictators served the vested interests of capital.

In the seventh chapter, Wells took off his gloves and told us straight out. In the Open Conspiracy the real or nominal rule of the king, the governing class, or the majority—monarchy, oligarchy, or democracy—would be replaced by "an effective criticism having the quality of science" and by "the growing will in men to have things right" (p. 73, below). Stirring words. But who would ensure that the men who thought they had things right would tolerate the free play of criticism? Who would guard the guardians?

Wells could not have answered. He had long since rejected democracy. Indeed, only one year after the 1931 edition of *The Open Conspiracy*, he published a collection of essays and lectures under the ominous title of *After Democracy*, in which he wrote, "I am asking for a Liberal Fascisti, for enlightened Nazis; I am proposing that you consider the formation of a greater Communist Party, a Western response to Russia."[25] Even in *The Outline of History*, written for a much less select public in a more liberal moment, he had listed the following as one of the fundamental principles of the coming world state:

> (vi) The world's political organization will be democratic, that is to say, the government and direction of affairs will be in immediate touch with and responsive to the general thought of the educated whole population.[26]

Read carefully. He did not say the world government would be elected by the people, or that it would even be responsive to the people—just to those who were "educated." More significantly, he gave not the least indication anywhere in the pages of *The Open Conspiracy* that it would be a democratically responsible movement or that its world state would practice either direct or electoral democracy.

I nurse no illusions about the integrity or efficiency of modern bourgeois democracy. As for socialist democracy, I have yet to see any major examples of it in sustained action. Leninism-Stalinism was never anything but autocratic state capitalism. Democracy does not exist in the People's Republic of China. But for all its flaws and failings, for all its vulnerability to corruption and subversion, democracy must go hand in hand with socialism, or there will never be a just socialist polity anywhere in the world. The people are not always right, but who is? And who else is socialism of, by, and for?

7. A Critical Assessment: Positive

I think you will agree that these are substantial criticisms of *The Open Conspiracy* and much of the rest of Wells's literary output. You may even wonder what I could say in favour of Wells's Conspiracy after everything you have just read. Not to worry. Serious as my objections may be, they are overshadowed, at least in my own mind, by the areas of assent and agreement that I shall now enumerate. The flaws of this book are more than compensated for by its tremendous strengths.

As I had seven problems, so I can offer seven affirmations, which may take less space to report, but are just as deeply felt. Again, I shall present them in reverse order of importance.

First, I fully agree with Wells in his third and fourth chapters that there can be no effective Open Conspiracy without a massive educational effort, both in formal schooling and in the media of communication. Such an effort must, as he insisted, strive to instill world-mindedness, to stretch brains and widen horizons. As a boy I was luckily exposed in elementary school to studies of pre-historic societies and world history. On my own initiative, I wrote a little book at the age of eight or nine entitled *The Earth and Its History*, which reviewed all the eras of geological time and told the story of the evolution of life. I did not learn about the history of my own city or county or state or nation. I learned about paleontology and Homo sapiens and the earth on which my species had flourished for tens of thousands of years. A bit later, thanks to the gift of a toy chemistry set, articles in the *National Geographic*, and Wells's *The Outline of History* and *The Science of Life* (both on the family bookshelf [27]), I was also moved to write "textbooks" of chemistry and ocean life, and plays about the Greco-Persian wars. None of these writings was of the slightest value to anyone else, but they remain as documents of a child whose brain was stretched and whose horizons were widened.

I like to call this curriculum I absorbed in my childhood "world studies." Not women's studies, gay studies, African studies, or European studies, but studies about the whole world, which manifestly includes women, gays, Africans, Europeans, and everything and everybody else on the broad face of our wondrous planet. If only a substantial proportion of the inhabitants of Terra could be programmed to think terrestrially, they would be ripe for the Open Conspiracy.

My second affirmation concerns the emphasis Wells placed on world bio-logical controls in various chapters of *The Open Conspiracy*, especially in the eighth and fourteenth. In this regard as in many others, Wells was far ahead of his time. With the earth's human population standing at just under two billion, alarm about the global "population explosion" was still largely a thing of the future, but Wells could see what was coming: steadily increasing pressure of demand upon supply, leading to the eventual exhaustion of earth's resources. Birth control had become essential, throughout the planet, along with conser-vation of wildlife and concerted efforts to reduce or eliminate disease. Had he lived longer, H.G. Wells would have been at the forefront of those urging planet-wide action to save the entire ecosystem from pollution and global warming. In both *The Science of Life* and *The Work, Wealth and Happiness of Mankind*, he defined economics as a branch of the science of ecology and warned that during the past two centuries humankind had been engaged in "a breeding storm" that might already be too late to stop. "Even now the human population may have passed the security point and be greater than it should be for a prosperous sustained biological equilibrium."[28]

I also have no problem, quite the reverse, with his declarations in the ninth and nineteenth chapters of *The Open Conspiracy* that the arrival of the world commonweal would mark not the end of the human story but only a stage along the way to far greater and wider adventures. I may have no "faith" in science, but it is a safe guess that science, technology, and engineering—including biological and molecular engineering—will furnish our species with the means to extend its powers almost beyond comprehension during the centuries, millennia, and eons that stretch out before us. Providing we survive our own greed and stupidity.

Seeing our blue Earth from the surface of the Moon, as we have now done, an Earth floating in the firmament like a precious jewel, reminds us of how incredibly beautiful and yet how fragile and vulnerable our world is. It also makes us appreciate all the more keenly the vastness of the cosmos. The nearly limitless space and time and energy of the universe shrink human achievement thus far to the dimensions of a single grain of sand on a thousand-mile-long beach. What could we not do, and see, and learn, in all that time and space, with all that energy at our call? I can even foresee an era when the human race will have long since outgrown its need for world commonweals and evolved into a hundred new species inhabiting numberless worlds. But not if we bungle our way through the 21st century as we did through the 20th. Not if we muff our chances in the here and now. There can never be a future without a past.

My fourth area of agreement with Wells is his provision in *The Open Conspiracy* and other texts, especially *The Shape of Things To Come*, for armed resistance to the sovereign state system and its corporate manipulators if and when such resistance became both possible and necessary. His Conspirators would need a military capability should things go from bad to worse, as he said plainly in the tenth and eighteenth chapters of *The Open Conspiracy*. I regret that he left us dangling with no details about how armed forces could be raised, equipped, and paid for. In *The Shape of Things To Come* he provided one possible scenario of military action used to speed and safeguard the transition to a peaceful world order, but only in the aftermath of an imaginary world war even more destructive than the real World War Two. Many other scenarios are conceivable, including the one he invented for World War One in *The War That Will End War*. The swords raised against Germany, he had written, were raised to put an end to the idiocy of militarism and build a postwar world state. On that occasion Wells was fooling himself. But "the war that will end war" was an idea well worth trying to sell, and which of us does not wish that he had made his sale?

In any case Wells did at least raise the possibility in *The Open Conspiracy* that the nation-states of his era would not "go gentle into that good night." A bloodless world revolution would be lovely, but the course of world history offered no guarantee of such a happy ending. It might be necessary to fight, and not just metaphorically, for the right of humankind to live together in peace.

I also, and with all possible enthusiasm, endorse Wells's appeal for the emergence of a new secular religion of humanity, as developed in his fifth and sixth chapters. I would go further and call it a religion of the service of being and becoming, of life itself and progress to a life more abundant. As Wells understood, immortality belongs to the species, not to the self (see p. 114, below). Our only hope of dodging death is to leave something of ourselves behind—our good works, our progeny, our place in the hearts of others. This is indeed religion, and without religion we are simply creatures of the moment, subject to every whim of our hormones, predators without grace, beasts of the field.

But Wells had no use for the positive religions of the past, with their pantheons of lofty imaginary beings, mystic fervours, promises of personal paradise, and brittle codes of right conduct. Many of the brightest men and women of our time cling to these religions *faute de mieux*. Many others believe that the bonds of ordinary society would dissolve without their ministrations. Such a belief insults the intelligence of all of us. And since there are dozens of traditional religious faiths in mortal conflict with one another throughout the world, they too often serve to divide, not unite, our frazzled species. I stand foursquare with Marx, Nietzsche, Freud, Russell, and Wells. For me, the gods of old are dead. They cannot be resurrected. Do we still need their opiates?

Yet we do need religious faith. I cannot imagine anyone giving himself or herself wholeheartedly to the cause of the Open Conspiracy, to the building of a great new world civilization, without a deep and abiding faith in human destiny. Why should an irreligious man or woman bother? Why should anyone without religious faith sacrifice the pleasures of the day for the well-being of future generations? Saul of Tarsus was mistaken. Faith, hope, and charity are not to be ranked: they are one and the same.

And let us be open-hearted. In the name of faith, hope, and charity, the Open Conspiracy must no doubt find a place in its ranks for men and women of good will who cannot forswear all of their older allegiances. Perhaps secular humanism and older faiths and cultures can learn to co-exist. In this respect, Wells was no doubt too Procrustean, too sure of himself, too unsparing.

My sixth affirmation of Wells touches on the same topic as my sixth objection to Wells: his socialism. Although I cannot accept his anti-Marxist views on class struggle, I do endorse his demand for the transfer of the ownership of several key categories of capital from private hands to duly constituted world authorities. This is absolutely essential not only to provide a more equitable distribution of wealth but also to make global democracy possible. The right to vote for one's leaders is almost meaningless if one is a slave to the iron laws of the capitalist market place. The right to elect one set of capitalists whose self-interest may be a tad more enlightened than the self-interest of another set, is a right almost not worth the trouble to exercise.

I also agree with Wells that among the categories of capital slated for transfer should be capital invested in credit, transport, staple production, land, and the world's waters. By "staple production," which Wells left vague, I mean the production and distribution of anything that the electorate considers essential to minimal standards of well-being under current conditions of civilized life. This might include most food and drink; home, office, and factory building materials and furnishings; clothing; fuels; pharmaceuticals; public schooling at all levels; banking services; electronic equipment necessary for productive work; as well as motor vehicles, trains, ships, aircraft, and spacecraft. The media of communications, whether postal, print, broadcast, or computerized, should be transferred to not-for-profit private foundations, independent from government in order to safeguard free speech and tribuneship.

But I would be inclined to exempt products still in an experimental stage of development and not yet mass marketed, as well as goods and services and retail sales facilities furnished by small companies hiring no more than, say, 25 employees. There is nothing wrong, and much good, in entrepreneurial activity as such. In my best judgement, freedom of enterprise is and should always remain a fundamental human right. A five-hectare vineyard producing premium Burgundy, a family-owned Chinese restaurant, a crafts shop making customized leather goods, or a small laboratory engaged in free-lance research are obvious examples of businesses that should be exempted from public ownership. However, when an entrepreneur possesses so much wealth and such a large share of the market that he or she can amass a huge personal fortune and buy and sell human labour at will, not to mention the favour of elected officials, that entrepreneur has crossed the line. He or she is guilty of what Wells called "the private monopolization of the sources of wealth" (p. 83, below). Such entrepreneurs inevitably come into conflict with the higher self-interest of humankind, as well as with the rights of other entrepreneurs, and must be retired on a generous pension or taxed out of business and returned to the market place to start all over again from zero.

This leaves us with my seventh and most critical affirmation of the message of *The Open Conspiracy*. I shall keep this very brief and very blunt. Whatever differences I may have with Wells, the basic project of an Open Conspiracy to lead our divided, bickering tribes to the Cosmopolis of an organic world civilization is the most urgent idea of our time. We must set about the task with no further delay. To paraphrase Wells, history becomes more and more a race between integration and catastrophe. There is no imaginable way to salvage the global environment, abolish armed conflict, ensure social and economic justice, and press forward to the discovery and settlement of the universe except by the mobilization of human will in a great new world commonweal. Such tasks are beyond the power of corporations, sovereign states, or benevolent societies. Self and local interest must yield to the interest of all humankind. Wells articulated this fundamental imperative more clearly and forcefully than any other thinker known to me, and that is why I believe *The Open Conspiracy* is the most important book written in the 20th century.

Part Three:

The Open Conspiracy Since Wells

1. The Post-Wellsian Generation, 1946-1970

H.G. Wells died on 13 August, 1946, in the house at 13 Hanover Terrace near Regent's Park in London where he had spent the war years, now and again ducking German bombs. Instead of ceremonies held throughout the world at local and regional headquarters of the Open Conspiracy, there was only a brief service at the Golders Green crematorium, attended by relatives and close friends.

The immediate postwar years, just like 1919 and 1920, were a period of extraordinary plasticity in world affairs. Displaced persons had to be resettled or returned to their homelands, relief measures organized on a massive scale, enemy territories occupied, regimes dismantled and replaced, peace conferences held, boundaries redrawn, colonial possessions relinquished or reconquered, and a new (and improved) League of Nations formed. It would have been a grand time for the Open Conspiracy, had the Open Conspiracy existed, to help shape the course of events.

In its absence, other initiatives were forthcoming. Movements lobbying for a union of the Atlantic democracies, for world federal government, for registries and constitutional conventions of world citizens, and various other cosmopolitan proposals sprang up and collected modest headlines for several years. There is still a World Federalist Movement with members in many countries, but the heyday of such initiatives came in the late 1940s.

1948 was an especially good year. At the University of Chicago, its *Wunderkind* chancellor Robert M. Hutchins and his Italian colleague Giuseppe Borgese had assembled a committee of eminent scholars to draft a World Constitution. The committee published its well-constructed draft with no little fanfare in 1948.[29] This was also the year that the United Nations adopted its Universal Declaration of Human Rights in Paris, a document still viewed by some as the keystone of any future world commonweal. It closely followed, and betrayed the influence of, the Sankey Declaration of the Rights of Man written (almost entirely) by Wells and distributed in several drafts and many languages throughout the world between 1940 and 1943.[30] The United Nations itself might be read—in its earliest years—as a quasi-Wellsian enterprise. From 1946 to 1948 the first Director General of UNESCO, its educational, social, and cultural agency, was Wells's old friend and co-author of *The Science of Life*, the distinguished biologist Julian Huxley.

A more explicitly Wellsian effort was put forward by the Hungarian nuclear physicist Leo Szilard. Perhaps the first scientist to realize the feasibility of a chain-reaction nuclear fission bomb, Szilard had persuaded Albert Einstein to broach the matter with President Franklin Roosevelt in 1939, an initiative that eventually led to the Manhattan Project and Hiroshima. In his reminiscences, Szilard reported that the creative spark for the idea of an atomic weapon came to him from reading Wells's 1914 novel *The World Set Free*, in which atomic bombs were fashioned from a radioactive isotope and used with devastating effect in a global war.[31] Szilard was also an admirer of *The Open Conspiracy* and had met Wells in 1929. The next year he formed a circle of scientists in Berlin to organize what he called simply *Der Bund*, a religious and scientific order of the best young minds, who would seek to wield a strong moral influence over political life. Whether *Der Bund* was directly inspired by *The Open Conspiracy* is not clear.[32] Its resemblance to the Order of Samurai proposed in Wells's much earlier work, *A Modern Utopia*, is even more striking. In any case, it never materialized.

After World War Two, remorseful for his role in uncorking the nuclear genie, Szilard decided once again to put flesh on the project of an Open Conspiracy, this time with some success. In 1962 he founded the Council for a Livable World (at first the Council for Abolishing War), an organization consisting largely of scientists whose task was to lobby for international cooperation and world peace and to support suitable peace candidates in U.S. election campaigns. Szilard died in 1964, but the Council outlived him and has done a measurable amount of good in the cosmopolitan cause.[33]

However, none of these endeavours was any real match for the Cold War, the bloody fission of India, the Arab-Israeli wars in the desecrated Holy Lands, Mao Zedong's successful armed revolution against the U.S.-supported Kuomintang regime in China, the military misadventures of the Western powers in Algeria and Korea and Indochina, the macabre thrills of the nuclear arms race, the Stalinist Gulag, or the Soviet tanks that rolled into Budapest and Prague. Hell continued to break loose. The polite, well-intentioned, mostly upper middle-class ladies and gentlemen who earnestly petitioned their legislators and fellow citizens to convert the United Nations into a world federation or end the nuclear arms race or counsel caution in high circles of government could do little to put out the flames.

More impressive in some ways than the various postwar peace movements were the visions of a new generation of social philosophers who stepped forward between the mid-1940s and about 1970 to preach, if not an Open Conspiracy, at least the imminence of a syncretic world civilization that would lay the moral, spiritual, and cultural foundations for Cosmopolis. Julian Huxley was among them. So were the historian Arnold J. Toynbee, the humanist Lewis Mumford, the philosopher F.S.C. Northrop, the sociologist Pitirim A. Sorokin, the Jesuit bio-mystic Pierre Teilhard de Chardin, and quite a few others. I have traced the course of their thought in *The City of Man*.[34] The otherworldly religiosity of many of these writers might have nauseated Wells, but I think he would also have found much to applaud in their priorities. It was the scientific humanist Huxley, after all, who liked Teilhard de Chardin well enough to write the Introduction to the English-language edition of the Frenchman's most important book, *The Phenomenon of Man* (1959).

The only problem with the "City of Man" philosophers is that their advocacy of a global civilization failed just as egregiously as Wells's Open Conspiracy and postwar world federalism to make any sort of serious dent either in public consciousness or in the conduct of world affairs. Some of the thinkers themselves were quite popular, for a while, in particular Toynbee and Teilhard. But not because they advocated Cosmopolis. They attracted attention and followers for other reasons, and then mostly faded from view altogether.

2. From 1970 to the End of the Century

Worse was yet to come. The last 30 years have seen the almost total collapse of cosmopolitanism, in the Wellsian sense. The world federalist movement has grayed and waned, without disappearing altogether. Proposals to transform the United Nations into something approaching a world government are rarely made and less often discussed. The U.N. itself has turned out better than the League of Nations, but remains largely a talking shop, dominated by the major Western powers, with a budget smaller than the budgets of most American states. Marxism, in its prime always a force for world-revolutionary transformation, has followed the former Soviet bloc into oblivion except for a few embattled academicians here and there. The "City of Man" philosophers discussed above are all dead and, by and large, forgotten.

One reason for the steep decline of cosmopolitanism has been the equally steep ascent of other ideologies and faiths with segmental interests that have managed to divert our attention from the general human predicament. These rival allegiances usually have concrete results to show for their efforts, which reinforces the belief of their followers that the old cosmopolitanism was utopian and impracticable. I am thinking now of movements for the empowerment of racial and religious minorities, women, gays and Lesbians, and oppressed ethnic groups (such as Kurds, Basques, or Hutus), as well as movements aiming at the revival of traditional religious faiths and cultures threatened by the secularist agenda of the modern Western world.

Mark well. The great majority of such movements have legitimate grievances and all kinds of reasons to take alarm and take action. But the net effect of their zeal has been to transfer attention from global to local or segmental concerns; and where they have been more or less successful, sometimes merely to make the existing world order work with less friction, as when women and persons of colour have been co-opted into the ruling class. They have also benefitted parochial and traditional cultural values at the expense of a cosmopolitan world-view. Meanwhile, the sovereign state system endures and proliferates, oligopoly capital bestrides the global market place, and the prospects for a Wellsian world commonweal retreat into some unimaginably distant era.

Another force militating against cosmopolitanism has been the rise of the so-called postmodern sensibility, with its distrust of "totalizing metanarratives" (such as the vision of world history expounded by Wells in *The Outline of History*). Postmodernism challenges the truth claims of all sciences, ideological and metaphysical world-views, and, indeed, the possibility of any sort of public philosophy. The followers of Derrida, Foucault, Lacan, and Lyotard must, in all conscience, scorn the confident rhetoric of an H.G. Wells, not to mention the metanarratives of the "City of Man" folk, consigning such delusions to one of the lowest circles of the postmodernist inferno. For them, all talk of cosmopolitanism may smack of fascist tyranny, ruthless homogenization of difference, Eurocentric white hegemony, or worse. And for those who have not been captured by the postmodernist rebellion, there is always the New Age, with its many-ring circus of gurus, psychics, messiahs, and healers, all eager to transport us to their various nirvanas, if we can afford the price of the ticket.

Of course now and then matches have been struck that illuminate the ambient gloom. I have already mentioned the futures studies movement, which grew from almost nothing in the mid-1960s to a thriving concern in the next few decades. Futurists are not of one mind or belief-system, to say the least, but the mere fact that most of them try to imagine what the world will be like, and should be like, in the future forces them to grapple with issues on a Wellsian scale. Unfortunately, only a handful of first-rate minds have been drawn thus far to futures studies and the discipline itself has failed to take significant root in the groves of academe. Moreover, all too many futurists are either sociologically impaired technological optimists, supporters of the economic and political status quo, or loopy New Agers.

A technological revolution with far-reaching implications for world integration that few futurists anticipated is the almost sudden emergence in the 1980s and 1990s of a global electronic information and communications system, still in its infancy but surely capable of realizing another dream of H.G. Wells. Electronic mail and worldwide internets and webs have put ordinary citizens of all countries in immediate touch with one another and with geometrically expanding databases, foreseen at least in part in Wells's 1938 book *World Brain* and further developed by Alan Mayne in the boldly imaginative Critical Introduction to his recent re-issue of *World Brain* itself.[35]

Another movement of the past 30 years that runs counter to the prevailing parochialism is environmentalism, the quest for a "sustainable future." Because environmentalists routinely think in terms of global problems, such as climate change, species extinctions, overpopulation, threats to the oceanic food chain, loss of wetlands and tropical forests, and ozone layer depletion, they help to fix the attention of the general public and of governments and corporations alike on concerns that necessarily cross national boundary lines. Environment- alist organizations from Greenpeace and the German Green Party (as well as its counterparts in other countries) to Lester R. Brown's impressive Worldwatch Institute in Washington appeal to the conscience of all humankind. Their chief shortcoming, which in another sense is their chief strength, is their tendency to avoid any real challenge to global capitalism and the sovereign state system. This is a strength, because it enables them to con- centrate all their energies on a single set of global issues. From the Wellsian perspective, it is also a grave weakness, as expounded in the parable of Provinder Island in the sixteenth chapter of *The Open Conspiracy*. Environmental issues, like virtually every great issue roiling humankind today, are linked to many others—economic, political, even spiritual. They can rarely be solved in isolation from one another.

Further cosmopolitan light has been shed in the closing decades of the 20th century by various small circles of scholars in the social sciences. The two best known to me are the World Policy Institute (formerly the World Law Fund) in New York and the international movement in sociology devoted to the study of "world-systems," growing from a seminal volume by the Binghamton University sociologist Immanuel Wallerstein, *The Modern World- System* (1974). The single most ambitious undertaking of the World Policy Institute has been its World Order Models Project, which produced a series of volumes on the desirable future world order by international teams of eminent scholars in the 1970s.[36] My *Building the City of Man* (1971) was published under the auspices of the World Policy Institute. For its part, the world-systems movement has generated a great number of excellent studies—totalizing meta- narratives that defy the strictures of postmodernist dogma—and some have come very near at times to the Wellsian vision of a socialist world common- weal. As Wallerstein has written, "Socialism involves the creation of a new kind of *world*-system, neither a redistributive world-empire nor a capitalist world-economy but a socialist world-government."[37]

Again, however, it cannot be argued that these or other like-spirited enter- prises have exerted a significant impact on the public mind or have accelerat- ed the process of world integration. They have done what they could, but their numbers are few, and they have won virtually no access to the literate multi- tudes of humankind outside small and select precincts of academe.

One could maintain, of course, that a new world order is in the works that owes little or nothing to the visions of scholars or the toils of activists. This has been, in effect, the thesis of Francis Fukuyama, much-acclaimed author of *The End of History and the Last Man* (1992). Fukuyama contends that with the end of the Cold War, the downfall of the Soviet Union and its bloc of satellites, and the obsolescence of Marxism, the more advanced segments of human civilization have left "history" behind—history defined as armed and ideological conflict among leading-edge nations. The field of battle has been cleared, and the winner is liberal democratic capitalism, a global system without major rivals or peers.

In effect, therefore, Fukuyama asserts that a new world civilization has already emerged. Many parts of Latin America, Africa, and Asia still do not share fully in its blessings, and are engaged in a variety of benighted struggles of the old historical sort. But the hope is that they, too, in good time, will leave history and join the club of the elect, to live happily ever after in peace, freedom, and prosperity. Benjamin Barber puts the same matter in a darker light in his *Jihad Vs. McWorld* (1995), noting that humanity is now in the throes of a monumental struggle between the centrifugal passions of separatism and the centripetal forces of global integration emanating from the megacorporate West, which promises to generate much drama and misery in the years ahead. Samuel P. Huntington has provoked lively controversy with his perversely brilliant analysis of the global problematique, *The Clash of Civilizations and the Remaking of World Order* (1996). In all these works, the central idea is that the Western world has arrived at some sort of millennium, at least in its own eyes, but must warily leave the rest of *Homo sapiens*, within "reason," to its own devices.

The trouble is that all these analyses of Western civilization are, in effect, endorsements of a world-system of piratical oligopoly capitalism and armed sovereign nation-states, in which the non-Western nations play a subordinate but ultimately loyal role, whether they know it or not and whether they wish it or not. A global capitalist market place welded to a nation-state system, the formula that has worked so well for Western capitalism since the 16th century, is not the Wellsian new world order. In texts such as *The World of William Clissold*, Wells hoped that somehow the trick could be done. He rhapsodized about the chance that a great outburst of world-mindedness would transform the moguls of multinational capital into angels. All we can say, today, is that most of these moguls are world-minded, to be sure, but not in the sense dreamed of by Wells. If they have set humankind on the path to a world civilization, it will be a world civilization for the rich, the privileged, and the rapacious, the ancestors of the beautiful people he satirized as the Eloi, the prize cattle of the terrifying far-future world in *The Time Machine*.

Meanwhile, history continues. The balance-sheet for the last three decades of the 20th century shows, I think, a large deficit for cosmopolitanism and a corresponding credit for every force in modern history that strives to keep all of us separate, conflicted, and enserfed. The house of earth is a house divided against itself. It will not stand.

3. The Idea of a World Party

A reviewer in the journal *Science-Fiction Studies* not long ago identified two social scientists who approach H.G. Wells's writings "as living political documents." One of them, Leon Stover, is an anthropologist who views the political Wells as a sort of Antichrist. The other is W. Warren Wagar, a historian, who of course does not. I accept the compliment with pleasure.[38] To me, the writings of Wells are indeed living political documents. They are the subject of my Ph.D. dissertation at Yale, which was entitled "The Open Conspirator: H.G. Wells as a Prophet of World Order." They are the subject of my first and third books, and of dozens of articles and reviews I have written in later years.[39] They are also the most direct inspiration for my own essays in prophecy and cosmopolitan advocacy.[40] In fact the title of my scenario-novel, *A Short History of the Future*, is a phrase that Wells used to describe his scenario-novel, *The Shape of Things To Come*.[41]

My personal version of the Open Conspiracy is what I have been calling for some 30 years the World Party, first discussed at length in *Building the City of Man* in 1971 and then assigned the starring role, so to speak, in *A Short History of the Future*.[42] No such party has ever come into existence, and perhaps never will, but it is my Open Conspiracy and I have not wavered in the conviction that something like it will be necessary to guide humankind to Cosmopolis.

In essence the idea of a World Party is the idea of a global political and cultural movement dedicated to the peaceful supersession (where possible) and the forceful surgical removal (where necessary) of the principal components of the present-day world-system. Root and branch. No half measures. No compromises, except for short-term tactical purposes. These principal components are the sovereign state system, with its doctrine of the priority of self-defined "vital" national interests, and the multinational corporations that own and manage most of the oligopolistic global economy.

Three overriding considerations lead me to conclude that this world-system must go. First, the sovereign states by their very nature cannot bring lasting peace and security to a world such as ours, riven by vast differences of wealth, human and natural resources, history, and culture. Second, self-interest prevents the sovereign states and corporate giants from being able to avert the ecological disasters menacing our planet in the 21st century. Third, the global economy is increasingly falling into the hands of a shrinking number of ever wealthier and more powerful brontosaurian corporate entities. Their ruthless commitment to the growth-and-profit dynamics of capitalism steadily narrows the access of most men and women to entrepreneurial opportunities and widens the gulf between the rich and the poor both within and among nations.

I realize that most of the intelligent and well educated people on our earth today do not accept these premises. Those who argue that globalizing forces have already begun and will continue to erode the sovereignty of independent states have a point. But the states and their armed forces persist, ready to resume major internecine warfare whenever their vital national interests are endangered by tensions and troubles in the world-system.

Those who argue that governments and corporations working together in their own enlightened self-interest can solve our environmental problems have a point, too. But will they actually do so, and do so in time, and without grave irreparable damage to the planetary ecosystem? I wager not.

Those who argue that capitalism produces so much wealth that there will always be enough to spread around no matter how much of it accumulates at the top may be right. But I think they are dead wrong. The logic of capitalism is to buy cheap and sell dear. The system ensures that there will always be winners and losers. Its long-term future can only involve the relative immiseration of labour, the super-enrichment of capital, and the annihilation of the so-called middle class, which is to say the "upper" stratum of the working class. There are abundant signs of this already in one of the world's most successful capitalist nations, the United States of America. Since the mid-1970s, the top 20% of Americans, as measured by income, have grown steadily more affluent, the bottom 20% steadily poorer, and those in the middle have either lost ground or gained very little. Moreover, of those in the highest quintile the top 10% have done better than those immediately below them, the top 5% better still, and the top 1% best of all.

How can a World Party accomplish the supersession or removal of the most powerful forces and institutions in today's world? This Critical Introduction is not the place to answer such an immense question. I have tried to answer it in the texts cited above. Let me just say that the World Party will need to engage in activities at all the levels recommended by Wells in *The Open Conspiracy*: political, social, economic, educational, and spiritual. Its members will at some early point elaborate a clear, commonsense religion of the world integration of humankind, a religion not of gods or miracles, but of wholehearted devotion to the progress of this remarkable biological species to which all of us without exception belong. The Party will preach and teach and illuminate. It will work to form alternative institutions, such as schools, producer and consumer co-operatives, and electronic networks linking its members all over the globe. It will run candidates for public office. It will organize militias competent to incite popular insurrections and mount armed resistance to state power when no other path is open. It will work in the light of day where and when it can. It will work below ground where and when it must. It will become, in the fullness of time, and after long struggles, the World Republic.

My vision differs from Wells's only in the ways discussed earlier. That is, I do not expect, as he did, that the World Party will originate and act primarily in the Atlantic nations. It must have sections and cadres throughout the world. It will also need to elect leaderships both regionally and globally and maintain a high level of internal organizational discipline and efficiency. Wells's aversion to a vertebrate Conspiracy is one I do not share, not for philosophical reasons but simply because I do not believe that human beings can work together effectively in unstructured associations. Would that they could!

Above all, the World Party will need to submit itself and justify itself to the mass of the world's people through the ballot box. Admittedly this may not be possible in some parts of the world until after mundialization has actually been achieved and the World Republic is in place. Thereafter, the Party will continue to hold itself accountable to the world's people and will compete democratically with any other political formations that arise to challenge it. In short, the coming of the World Republic spells not the end of politics, as Wells anticipated, but its ascent to a higher plane, freed from the malodorous manipulations of big capital. The World Republic will be ruled not by science or expertise, invaluable as these things may be, but by the minds of all humankind, by what Jean-Jacques Rousseau called more than two centuries ago the "General Will." This great Will must remain at all times the only true sovereign power on earth.

4. Prospects

What are the chances that Wells's Open Conspiracy or my World Party or any other institution or force or combination of efforts and circumstances can bring humankind to Cosmopolis in the 21st century—or, for that matter, in the 22nd or 23rd, or ever?

The odds are, I think, very much against us. One hundred years of propaganda for a just world state on the part of H.G. Wells and his successors have so far led nowhere. True, humanity is more unified today than it was at the beginning of Wells's prophetic mission. The major states of Western and Central Europe, for example, are no longer engaged in their millennium-long struggle to conquer one another. Capitalist globalization has fashioned a world economic community far more interdependent than ever before. But if what we want is a democratic and socialist government of all humankind dedicated to equality, freedom, and peace, then our various efforts have led nowhere. Wells did not succeed, nor did Gandhi and Nehru, nor Sun and Mao, nor Wilson and Roosevelt, nor Lenin and Gorbachev, nor King and Mandela. The parties of socialism, communism, liberalism, and anarchism have failed. We have all failed.

Must we always fail? I do not know. The Cosmopolis that seems so near at hand, so easily achievable given all we can do, given all our science, technology, and accumulated knowledge of ourselves, may be the most fragile of mirages, a will-o'-the-wisp, a fleck of foam on a passing wave. The established order, by contrast, looks as solid and impervious as Mount Everest. Established orders always do. The Han Dynasty, the Empire of Asoka, the Pax Romana, the France of Louis XIV and Napoleon, the Thousand-Year Third Reich. One of my favourite monuments in the world is the one I saw a few years ago in the eastern quarter of Berlin, engraved in German with the intoxicating slogan, "Long Live the Eternal Friendship of the Union of Soviet Socialist Republics and the German Democratic Republic!" By all means. For all we know, these worthy republics are hugging one another even now in some great Valhalla in the sky. But they are Established Orders no more.

So, yes, let us not be deceived by our own failures or the apparent strengths of others. Whatever human beings can do, they can undo, and make, and remake again. History teaches us little respect for the boasts of any state or system or class that has ever strutted on its stage. The Open Conspiracy has not yet made its own entrance. It may never win the chance. But what else are we to do with our lives? How else can we justify our existence to our fellow men and women? To what tribal totem or dead god or moss-grown myth should we genuflect instead? Read *The Open Conspiracy*. Decide for yourselves.

Endnotes

1 For sales figures, see W. Warren Wagar, *H.G. Wells and the World State*. New Haven and London: Yale University Press, 1961, p. 186, fn 40.

2 Some of its first classics were Bertrand de Jouvenel, *The Art of Conjecture* [1964], New York: Basic Books, 1967; Herman Kahn and Anthony J. Wiener, *The Year 2000: A Framework for Speculation on the Next Thirty-Three Years*, New York: Macmillan, 1967; John McHale, *The Future of the Future*, New York: George Braziller, 1969; and Daniel Bell, *The Coming of Post-Industrial Society: A Venture in Social Forecasting*, New York: Basic Books, 1973. Its first best seller was Alvin Toffler's *Future Shock*, New York: Random House, 1970. Its most significant journals, de Jouvenel's *Futuribles* in Paris, Edward Cornish's *The Futurist* in Washington, and the leading British journal, *Futures*, all got their starts in 1966-68, and are still going strong at this writing [1997].

3 David C. Smith, *H.G. Wells, Desperately Mortal: A Biography*. New Haven and London: Yale University Press, 1986, p. 96.

4 H.G. Wells, *The Discovery of the Future* [1902], ed. Patrick Parrinder. London: PNL Press, 1989, p. 27.

5 Wells, "Wanted—Professors of Foresight!" [1932], *Futures Research Quarterly*, 3 (Spring 1987), 90-91.

6 W. Warren Wagar, *The Next Three Futures: Paradigms of Things To Come*. New York: Praeger Publishers, 1991; and London: Adamantine Press, 1992, pp. 15-23. See also my article, "Futurism," in George Thomas Kurian and Graham T.T. Molitor, *Encyclopedia of the Future*. New York: Macmillan Library Reference, 1996, I:366-367.

7 Wells, *A Year of Prophesying*. New York: Macmillan, 1925, pp. 33, 61, and 104.

8 *Ibid.*, p. 109.

9 Wells, *Anticipations of the Reaction of Mechanical and Scientific Progress Upon Human Life and Thought*. New York: Harper, 1902, p. 190.

10 Wells, *The Passionate Friends*. New York: Harper, 1913, p. 273.

11 Wells, *The War That Will End War*. New York: Duffield, 1914, pp. 67-68.

12 Wells, *Experiment in Autobiography: Discoveries and Conclusions of a Very Ordinary Brain (Since 1866)*. New York, Macmillan, 1934, p. 705.

13 Wells, *The Open Conspiracy: Blue Prints for a World Revolution*. Garden City, NY: Doubleday, Doran, 1928, p. vii.

14 Wells, *The Outline of History: Being a Plain History of Life and Mankind*. New York: Macmillan, 1920, II:594.

15 The reference to "republican Germany" was dropped in the 1935 *Thinker's Library* edition, the only way in which this edition differs significantly from the edition of 1931.

16 A no less ambitious effort was *Phoenix: A Summary of the Inescapable Conditions of World Reorganisation*. London: Secker and Warburg, 1942. With World War Two in full swing, here the Open Conspiracy had become the World Revolutionary Movement, and Wells pinned his hopes on postwar actions by the victorious Allied powers. When they had finally dealt with "the Fascist gangster adventure," they would have to set up special commissions to administer the peace. These commissions, if the Movement did its work well, would gradually be transformed into world authorities with powers delegated by the various national governments. In due course the national governments would lose their usefulness and fade out of existence. See especially pp. 180-182.

17 Wagar, *H.G. Wells and the World State*, pp. 175-185.

18 See *ibid.*, p. 182, fn 35.

19 My "world state" books are *H.G. Wells and the World State, The City of Man: Prophecies of a World Civilization in Twentieth-Century Thought* (1963), *Building the City of Man: Outlines of a World Civilization* (1971), *The Next Three Futures: Paradigms of Things To Come* (1991), and *A Short History of the Future*, 2nd ed. (1992).

20 *The War That Will End War*, p. 22.

21 Wagar, *The City of Man: Prophecies of a World Civilization in Twentieth-Century Thought*. Boston: Houghton Mifflin, 1963, pp. 246-257.

22 I say as much in my article "H.G. Wells and the Radicalism of Despair," *Studies in the Literary Imagination*, 6 (Fall 1973), 1-10.

23 For a contrary view, see Leon Stover, *The Prophetic Soul: A Reading of H.G. Wells's Things to Come*. Jefferson, North Carolina, and London: McFarland, 1987.

24 For a fuller account, see my *H.G. Wells and the World State*, pp. 164-174, and also, in a more critical vein, my essay "Science and the World State: Education as Utopia in the Prophetic Vision of H.G. Wells," in Patrick Parrinder and Christopher Rolfe, eds., *H.G. Wells under Revision*. Selinsgrove, PA: Susquehanna University Press; and London and Toronto: Associated University Presses, 1990, pp. 40-53.

25 Wells, *After Democracy*. London: Watts, 1932, p. 24.

26 Wells, *The Outline of History*, II:587.

27 Two other books on that shelf that I read eagerly were *The Story of Mankind* (1921) and *Van Loon's Geography* (1932), by the Dutch-American writer Hendrik Willem van Loon. Wells always viewed van Loon as a worthy competitor in the business of stocking the public mind with the knowledge it needed for world citizenship. See p. 60, below.

28 Wells, *The Work, Wealth and Happiness of Mankind*. Garden City, NY: Doubleday, Doran, 1931, I:210-211.

29 Committee To Frame a World Constitution, *Preliminary Draft of a World Constitution*. Chicago: University of Chicago Press, 1948. See also G.A. Borgese, *Foundations of the World Republic*. Chicago: University of Chicago Press, 1953.

30 A convenient place to find the final draft of Wells's declaration is Appendix C of Smith, *H.G. Wells, Desperately Mortal*, pp. 490-492. Smith tells the story of the Rights of Man campaign at length in his Chapter 17. See also Wells, *The Rights of Man; or, What Are We Fighting For?*, a Penguin Special published in 1940; and Wells,

Phoenix, pp. 186-192.

[31] Leo Szilard, *Leo Szilard: His Version of the Facts: Selected Recollections and Correspondence*, eds. Spencer R. Weart and Gertrud Weiss Szilard. Cambridge, Massachusetts, and London: M.I.T. Press, 1978, pp. 16 and 18.

[32] *Ibid.*, pp. 22-30. See especially p. 22, fn 2.

[33] A full account of Szilard's work as a peace activist is available in Michael Bess, *Realism, Utopia, and the Mushroom Cloud: Four Activist Intellectuals and Their Strategies for Peace, 1945-1989*. Chicago: University of Chicago Press, 1993, ch. 2.

[34] *The City of Man*, chs. 2-5. Slightly revised and with a newly written Preface, *The City of Man* also appeared later as a paperback in the United States. Baltimore: Penguin Books, 1967.

[35] See Alan Mayne, "Critical Introduction," in H.G. Wells, *World Brain*, London: Adamantine Press, 1994, pp. 1-70.

[36] An abridged version of the volumes of the World Order Models Project is available in Saul H. Mendlovitz, ed., *On the Creation of a Just World Order*. New York: Free Press, 1975. The most explicitly Wellsian of these volumes is Richard A. Falk, *A Study of Future Worlds*. New York: Free Press, 1975.

[37] Immanuel Wallerstein, *The Capitalist World-Economy*. Cambridge and London: Cambridge University Press, 1979, p. 35. Major books produced by world-systems scholars include Wallerstein, *The Modern World-System: Capitalist Agriculture and the Origins of the European World-Economy in the Sixteenth Century*, San Diego: Academic Press, 1974; Wallerstein, *The Modern World-System II: Mercantilism and the Consolidation of the European World-Economy, 1600-1750*, New York: Academic Press, 1980; Wallerstein, *The Modern World-System III: The Second Era of Great Expansion of the Capitalist World-Economy, 1730-1840s*, San Diego: Academic Press, 1989; Giovanni Arrighi, *The Long Twentieth Century: Money, Power, and the Origins of Our Times*, London and New York: Verso, 1994; Christopher Chase-Dunn, *Global Formation: Structures of the World-Economy*, Oxford and Cambridge, Massachusetts: Blackwell, 1989; Christopher Chase-Dunn and Thomas D. Hall, *Rise and Demise: Comparing World-Systems*, Boulder, Colorado: Westview Press, 1997; Stephen K. Sanderson, *Social Transformations: A General Theory of Historical Development*, Oxford and Cambridge, Massachusetts: Blackwell, 1995; and Andre Gunder Frank and Barry K. Gills, eds., *The World System: Five Hundred Years or Five Thousand?*, London and New York: Routledge, 1993. Wallerstein also wrote the Afterword to my own *A Short History of the Future* (1989), Chicago: University of Chicago Press, 2nd ed., 1992, pp. 295-296; and see my article, "Socialism, Nationalism, and Ecocide," in the journal of Wallerstein's Fernand Braudel Center, *Review*, 19 (Summer 1996), 319-333.

[38] David Y. Hughes, "The Doctor Vivisected," *Science-Fiction Studies*, 24 (March 1997), 117, n 1. Stover's attack on the Open Conspiracy in the guise it takes in Wells's film *Things To Come* is cited above, n 22.

[39] *H.G. Wells and the World State* has already been cited. The third is Wagar, ed., *H.G. Wells: Journalism and Prophecy, 1893-1946*, an edited collection of excerpts from Wells's forecasts and commentaries on current affairs. Boston: Houghton Mifflin, 1964; and (revised) London: The Bodley Head, 1966.

[40] Cited above in n 18.

[41] Wells, *The Shape of Things To Come*. New York: Macmillan, 1933, p. 4.

[42] See Wagar, *Building the City of Man: Outlines of a World Civilization*, New York: Richard Grossman, 1971, pp. 57-67; and Wagar, *A Short History of the Future*, 2nd ed., Chicago: University of Chicago Press and London: Adamantine Press, 1992, especially pp. 43-44 and 134-145. For the record I had already written briefly about the need for a world party in "The Bankruptcy of the Peace Movement," *War/Peace Report*, 9 (August-September 1969), 3-6. This article was, in turn, a sympathetic response to an editorial in the same journal in its May 1968 issue, in which the editor had seconded the appeal of Labour Party leader Hugh Gaitskell (speaking in Paris in 1962) for a new World Party. Richard Hudson, "For a World Political Party," *War/Peace Report*, 8 (May 1968), 12-13. Hudson later returned to his idea in comments on a letter I sent him, published in the December 1968 issue. Agreeing with me that the national governments could not be relied upon to surrender their sovereignty voluntarily, Hudson continued: "This is precisely why I think an outside force—a World Political Party, or Movement, of individuals—is needed to push on the nation states and international organizations." In time such a Party might not only pressure states and international organizations but also seek "to achieve some power on the world level." *War/Peace Report*, 8 (December 1968), 24. In recent years a world party has also been proposed by political scientists writing in *Alternatives*, the journal of the World Order Models Project. See William P. Kreml and Charles W. Kegley, Jr., "A Global Political Party: The Next Step," *Alternatives: Social Transformation and Human Governance*, 21 (1996), 123-134.

THE OPEN CONSPIRACY

H.G. Wells

on

World Revolution

by H.G. Wells

The Open Conspiracy

I

The Present Crisis In Human Affairs

The world is undergoing immense changes. Never before have the conditions of life changed so swiftly and enormously as they have changed for mankind in the last fifty years. We have been carried along – with no means of measuring the increasing swiftness in the succession of events. We are only now beginning to realize the force and strength of the storm of change that has come upon us.

These changes have not come upon our world from without. No huge meteorite from outer space has struck our planet; there have been no overwhelming outbreaks of volcanic violence or strange epidemic diseases; the sun has not flared up to excessive heat or suddenly shrunken to plunge us into Arctic winter. The changes have come through men themselves. Quite a small number of people, heedless of the ultimate consequences of what they did, one man here and a group there, have made discoveries and produced and adopted inventions that have changed all the conditions of social life.

We are now just beginning to realize the nature of these changes, to find words and phrases for them and put them down. First they began to happen, and then we began to see that they were happening. And now we are beginning to see how these changes are connected together and to get the measure of their consequences. We are getting our minds so clear about them that soon we shall be able to demonstrate them and explain them to our children in our schools. We do not do so at present. We do not give our children a chance of discovering that they live in a world of universal change.

What are the broad lines upon which these alterations of condition are proceeding?

It will be most convenient to deal with them in the order in which they came to be realized and seen clearly, rather than by the order in which they came about or by their logical order. They are more or less interdependent changes; they overlap and interact.

It was only in the beginning of the twentieth century that people began to realize the real significance of that aspect of our changing conditions to which the phrase *"the abolition of distance"* has been applied. For a whole century before that there had been a continual increase in the speed and safety of travel

and transport and the ease and swiftness with which messages could be trans-
mitted, but this increase had not seemed to be a matter of primary importance.
Various results of railway, steamship, and telegraph became manifest; towns
grew larger, spreading into the countryside, once inaccessible lands became
areas of rapid settlement and cultivation, industrial centres began to live on
imported food, news from remote parts lost its time-lag and tended to become
contemporary, but no one hailed these things as being more than "improvements" in existing conditions. They are not observed to be the beginnings of a
profound revolution in the life of mankind. The attention of young people was
not drawn to them; no attempt was made, or considered necessary, to adapt
political and social institutions to this creeping enlargement of scale.

Until the closing years of the nineteenth century there was no recognition
of the real state of affairs. Then a few observant people began, in a rather tentative, commentary sort of way, to call attention to what was happening. They
did not seem to be moved by the idea that something had to be done about it;
they merely remarked, brightly and intelligently, that it was going on. And then
they went on to the realization that this "abolition of distance" was only one
aspect of much more far-reaching advances.

Men were travelling about so much faster and flashing their communications instantly about the world because a progressive conquest of force and
substance was going on. Improved transport was only one of a number of por-
tentous consequences of that conquest; the first to be conspicuous and set men
thinking; but not perhaps the first in importance. It dawned upon them that in
the last hundred years there had been a stupendous progress in obtaining and
utilizing mechanical power, a vast increase in the efficiency of mechanism, and
associated with that an enormous increase in the substances available for man's
purposes, from vulcanized rubber to the modern steels, and from petroleum
and margarine to tungsten and aluminium. At first the general intelligence was
disposed to regard these things as lucky "finds," happy chance discoveries. It
was not apprehended that the shower of finds was systematic and continuous.
Popular writers told about these things but they told of them at first as
"Wonders" – "Wonders" like the Pyramids, the Colossus of Rhodes, and the
Great Wall of China. Few realized how much more they were than any
"Wonders." The "Seven Wonders of the World" left men free to go on living,
toiling, marrying, and dying as they had been accustomed to for immemorial
ages. If the "Seven Wonders" had vanished or been multiplied three score it
would not have changed the lives of any large proportion of human beings. But
these new powers and substances were modifying and transforming – unob-
trusively, surely, and relentlessly – every particular of the normal life of
mankind.

They increased the amount of production and the methods of production.
They made possible "Big-Business," to drive the small producer and the small
distributor out of the market. They swept away factories and evoked new ones.
They changed the face of the fields. They brought into the normal life, thing

by thing and day by day, electric light and heating, bright cities at night, better aeration, new types of clothing, a fresh cleanliness. They changed a world where there had never been enough into a world of potential plenty, into a world of excessive plenty. It dawned upon their minds after their realization of the "abolition of distance" that shortage of supplies had also been abolished and that irksome toil was no longer necessary to produce everything material that man might require. It is only in the last dozen years that this broader and profounder fact has come through to the intelligence of any considerable number of people. Most of them have still to carry their realization a step farther and see how complete is the revolution in the character of the daily life these things involve.

But there are still other changes outside this vast advance in the pace and power of material life. The biological sciences have undergone a corresponding extension. Medical art has attained a new level of efficiency, so that in all the modernizing societies of the world the average life is prolonged, and there is, in spite of a great fall in the birth rate, a steady, alarming increase in the world's population. The proportion of adults alive is greater than it has ever been before. Fewer and fewer human beings die young. This has changed the social atmosphere about us. The tragedy of lives cut short and ended prematurely is passing out of general experience. Health becomes prevalent. The continual toothaches, headaches, rheumatism, neuralgias, coughs, colds, indigestions that made up so large a part of the briefer lives of our grandfathers and grandmothers fade out of experience. We may all live now, we discover, without any great burthen of toil or fear, wholesomely and abundantly, for as long as the desire to live is in us.

But we do not do so. All this possible freedom of movement, this power and abundance, remains for most of us no more than possibility. There is a sense of profound instability about these achievements of our race. Even those who enjoy, enjoy without security, and for the great multitude of mankind there is neither ease, plenty, nor freedom. Hard tasks, insufficiency, and unending money worries are still the ordinary stuff of life. Over everything human hangs the threat of such war as man has never known before, war armed and reinforced by all the powers and discoveries of modern science.

When we demand why the achievement of power turns to distress and danger in our hands, we get some very unsatisfactory replies. The favourite platitude of the politician, excusing himself for the futilities of his business, is that "moral progress has not kept pace with material advance." That seems to satisfy him completely, but it can satisfy no other intelligent person. He says "moral." He leaves that word unexplained. Apparently he wants to shift the responsibility to our religious teachers. At the most he has made but the vaguest gesture towards a reply. And yet, when we consider it, charitably and sympathetically, there does seem to be a germ of reality in that phrase of his.

What does moral mean? *Mores* means manners and customs. Morality is the conduct of life. It is what we do with our social lives. It is how we deal with ourselves in relation to our fellow creatures. And there does seem to be a much greater discord now than there was (say) a couple of hundred years ago between the prevailing ideas of how to carry on life and the opportunities and dangers of the time. We are coming to see more and more plainly that certain established traditions which have made up the frame of human relationships for ages are not merely no longer as convenient as they were, but are positively injurious and dangerous. And yet at present we do not know how to shake off these traditions, these habits of social behaviour which rule us. Still less are we able to state, and still less bring into operation, the new conceptions of conduct and obligation that must replace them.

For example, the general government of human affairs has hitherto been distributed among a number of sovereign states – there are about seventy of them now – and until recently that was a quite tolerable system of frameworks into which a general way of living could be fitted. The standard of living may not have been as high as our present standards, but the social stability and assurance were greater. The young were trained to be loyal, law-regarding, patriotic, and a defined system of crimes and misdemeanours with properly associated pains, penalties, and repressions, kept the social body together. Everyone was taught a history glorifying his own state, and patriotism was chief among the virtues. Now, with great rapidity, there has been that "abolition of distance," and everyone has become next-door neighbour to everyone else. States once separate, social and economic systems formerly remote from one another, now jostle each other exasperatingly. Commerce under the new conditions is perpetually breaking nationalist bounds and making militant raids upon the economic life of other countries. This exacerbates patriotism in which we have all been trained and with which we are all, with scarcely an exception, saturated. And meanwhile war, which was once a comparative slow bickering upon a front, has become war in three dimensions, it gets at the "non-combatant?" almost as searchingly as at the combatant, and has acquired weapons of a stupendous cruelty and destructiveness. At present there exists no solution to this paradoxical situation. We are continually being urged by our training and traditions to antagonisms and conflicts that will impoverish, starve, and destroy both our antagonists and ourselves. We are all trained to distrust and hate foreigners, salute our flag, stiffen up in a wooden obedient way at our national anthem, and prepare to follow the little fellows in spurs and feathers who pose as the heads of our states into the most horrible common destruction. Our political and economic ideas of living are out of date, and we find great difficulty in adjusting them and reconstructing them to meet the huge and strenuous demands of the new times. That is really what our gramophone politicians have in mind – in the vague way in which they have anything in mind – when they put on that well-worn record about moral progress not having kept pace with material inventions.

Socially and politically we want a revised system of ideas about conduct, a view of social and political life brought up to date. We are not doing the effective thing with our lives, we are drifting, we are being hoodwinked and bamboozled and misled by those who trade upon the old traditions. It is preposterous that we should still be followed about and pestered by war, taxed for war preparations, and threatened bodily and in our liberties by this unnecessary and exaggerated and distorted survival of the disunited world of the pre-scientific era. And it is not simply that our political way of living is now no better than an inherited defect and malformation, but that our everyday life, our eating and drinking and clothing and housing and going about, is also cramped, thwarted, and impoverished, because we do not know how to set about shaking off the old ways and fitting the general life to our new opportunities. The strain takes the form of increased unemployment and a dislocation of spending power. We do not know whether to spend or save. Great swarms of us find ourselves unaccountably thrown out of work. Unjustly, irrationally. Colossal business reconstructions are made to increase production and accumulate profits, and meanwhile the customers with purchasing power dwindle in numbers and fade away. The economic machine creaks and makes every sign of stopping – and its stopping means universal want and starvation. It must not stop. There must be a reconstruction, a change-over. But what sort of a change-over?

Though none of us are yet clear as to the precise way in which this great change-over is to be effected, there is a world-wide feeling now that change-over or a vast catastrophe is before us. Increasing multitudes participate in that uneasy sense of insecure transition. In the course of one lifetime mankind has passed from a state of affairs that seems to us now to have been slow, dull, ill-provided, and limited, but at least picturesque and tranquil minded, to a new phase of excitement, provocation, menace, urgency, and actual or potential distresses. Our lives are part of one another. We cannot get away from it. We are items in a social mass. What are we to do with our lives?

II

The Idea Of The Open Conspiracy

I am a writer upon social and political matters. Essentially I am a very ordinary, undistinguished person. I have a mediocre brain, a very average brain, and the way in which my mind reacts to these problems is therefore very much the way in which most brains will react to them. But because it is my business to write and think about these questions, because on that account I am able to give more time and attention to them than most people, I am able to get rather ahead of my equals and to write articles and books just a little before the ideas I experience become plain to scores of thousands, and then to hundreds of thousands, and at last to millions of other people. And so it happened that a few years ago (round about 1927) I became very anxious to clear up and give form to a knot of suggestions that seemed to me to have in them the solution of this riddle of adapting our lives to the immense new possibilities and the immense new dangers that confront mankind.

It seemed to me that all over the world intelligent people were waking up to the indignity and absurdity of being endangered, restrained, and impoverished, by a mere uncritical adhesion to traditional governments, traditional ideas of economic life, and traditional forms of behaviour, and that these awaking intelligent people must constitute first a protest and then a creative resistance to the inertia that was stifling and threatening us. These people I imagined would say first, "We are drifting; we are doing nothing worth while with our lives. Our lives are dull and stupid and not good enough."

Then they would say, "What are we to do with our lives?"

And then, "Let us get together with other people of our sort and make over the world into a great world-civilization that will enable us to realize the promises and avoid the dangers of this new time."

It seemed to me that as, one after another, we woke up, that is what we should be saying. It amounted to a protest, first mental and then practical, it amounted to a sort of unpremeditated and unorganized conspiracy, against the fragmentary and insufficient governments and the wide-spread greed, appropriation, clumsiness, and waste that are now going on. But unlike conspiracies in general this widening protest and conspiracy against established things would, by its very nature, go on in the daylight, and it would be willing to accept participation and help from every quarter. It would, in fact, become an "Open Conspiracy," a necessary, naturally evolved conspiracy, to adjust our dislocated world.

I made various attempts to develop this idea. I published a little book called *The Open Conspiracy* as early as 1928, into which I put what I had in my mind at that time. It was an unsatisfactory little book even when I published it, not quite plain enough and not quite confident enough, and evidently unsure of its readers. I could not find out how to do it better at the time, and it seemed in its way to say something of living and current interest, and so I published it – but I arranged things so that I could withdraw it in a year or so. That I did, and this present book is a largely rewritten version, much clearer and more explicit. Since that first publication we have all got forward surprisingly. Events have hustled thought along and have been hustled along by thought. The idea of reorganizing the affairs of the world on quite a big scale, which was "Utopian," and so forth, in 1926 and 1927, and still "bold" in 1928, has now spread about the world until nearly everybody has it. It has broken out all over the place, thanks largely to the mental stimulation of the Russian Five Year Plan. Hundreds of thousands of people everywhere are now thinking upon the lines foreshadowed by my Open Conspiracy, not because they had ever heard of the book or phrase, but because that was the way thought was going.

The first *Open Conspiracy* conveyed the general idea of a world reconstructed, but it was very vague about the particular way in which this or that individual life could be lived in relation to that general idea. It gave a general answer to the question, "What are we to do with our lives?" It said, "Help to make over the New World amidst the confusions of the Old." But when the question was asked, "What am *I* to do with my life?" the reply was much less satisfactory.

The intervening years of thought and experience make it possible, now, to bring this general idea of a reconstructive effort, an attempt to build up a new world within the dangers and disharmonies of our present state, into a much closer and more explicit relation to the individual "Open Conspirator." We can present the thing in a better light and handle it with a surer touch.

III

WE HAVE TO CLEAR AND CLEAN UP OUR MINDS

Now, one thing is fairly plain to most of us who are waking up to the need of living our lives in a new way and of making over the state, which is the framework of our lives, to meet the new demands upon it, and that is, that we have to put our own minds in order. Why have we only awakened now to the crisis in human affairs. The changes in progress have been going on with a steady acceleration for a couple of centuries. Clearly we must all have been very unobservant, our knowledge as it came to us must have been very badly arranged in our minds, and our way of dealing with it must have been cloudy and muddled, or else we should surely have awakened long ago to the immense necessities that now challenge us. And if that is so, if it has taken decades to rouse us, then quite probably we are not yet completely awake. Even now we may not have realized the job before us in its completeness. We may still have much to get plain in our minds, and we certainly have much more to learn. One primary and permanent duty therefore is to go on with our thinking and to think as well as we can about the way in which we think and about the ways in which we get and use knowledge.

Fundamentally the Open Conspiracy must be an intellectual rebirth.

Human thought is still very much confused by the imperfection of the words and other symbols it employs and the consequences of this confused thinking are much more serious and extensive than is commonly realized. We still see the world through a mist of words; it is only the things immediately about us that are plain fact. Through symbols, and especially through words, man has raised himself above the level of the ape and come to a considerable mastery over his universe. But every step in his mental ascent has involved entanglement with these symbols and words he was using; they were at once helpful and very dangerous and misleading. A great part of our affairs, social, political, intellectual, is in a perplexing and dangerous state to-day because of our loose, uncritical, slovenly use of words.

All through the later Middle Ages there were great disputes among the schoolmen about the use of words and symbols. There is a queer disposition in the human mind to think that symbols and words and logical deductions are truer than actual experiences, and these great controversies were due to the struggle of the human intelligence against that disposition. On the one side were the Realists, who were so called because they believed, in effect, that names were more real than facts, and on the other side were the Nominalists, who from the first were pervaded by a suspicion about names and words generally; who thought there might be some sort of catch in verbal processes, and who gradually worked their way towards *verification by experiment* which is the fundamental thing about experimental science – experimental science which has given our human world all these immense powers and possibilities that tempt and threaten it to-day. These controversies of the schoolmen were of the utmost importance to mankind. The modern world could not begin to come into existence until the human mind had broken away from the narrow-minded verbalist way of thinking which the Realists followed.

But all through my education I never had this matter explained to me. The University of London intimated that I was a soundly educated young man by giving me a degree in first-class honours and the liberty to acquire and wear an elegant gown and hood, and the London College of Preceptors gave me and the world its highest assurances that I was fit to educate and train the minds of my fellow creatures, and yet I had still to discover that a Realist was not a novelist who put rather too highly flavoured sex appeal into his books, and a Nominalist, nothing in particular. But it had crept into my mind as I learnt about individuality in my biological work and about logic and psychology in my preparation as the perfect preceptor, that something very important and essential was being left out and that I wasn't at all as well equipped as my diplomas presently said I was, and in the next few years I found the time to clean up this matter pretty thoroughly. I made no marvellous discoveries, everything I found out was known already; nevertheless, I had to find out some of this stuff for myself quite over again, as though it had never been done; so inaccessible was any complete account of human thinking to an ordinary man who wanted to get his mind into proper working condition. And this was not that I had missed some recondite, precious refinements of philosophy; it was that my fundamental thinking, at the very root of my political and social conduct, was wrong. I was in a human community, and that community, and I with it, was thinking of phantoms and fantasies as though they were real and living things, was in a reverie of unrealities, was blind, slovenly, hypnotized, base and ineffective, blundering about in an extremely beautiful and an extremely dangerous world.

I set myself to re-educate myself, and after the practice of writers wrote it in various trial pamphlets, essays, and books. There is no need to refer to these books here. The gist of the matter is set out in three compilations, to which I shall refer again almost immediately. They are *The Outline of History* (Ch. XXI, § 6, and Ch. XXXIII, § 6), *The Science of Life* (Book VIII, on Thought and Behaviour) and *The Work, Wealth, and Happiness of Mankind* (Ch. II, §§ 1-4). In the last, it is shown quite plainly how man has had to struggle for the mastery of his mind, has discovered only after great controversies the proper and effective use of his intellectual tools, and has had to learn to avoid certain widespread traps and pitfalls before he could achieve his present mastery over matter. Thinking clearly and effectively does not come by nature. Hunting the truth is an art. We blunder naturally into a thousand misleading generalizations and false processes. Yet there is hardly any intelligent mental training done in the schools of the world to-day. We have to learn this art, if we are to practise it at all. Our schoolteachers have had no proper training themselves, they mis-educate by example and precept, and so it is that our press and current discussions are more like an impromptu riot of crippled and deaf and blind minds than an intelligent interchange of ideas. What bosh one reads! What rash and impudent assumptions! What imbecile inferences!

But re-educating oneself, getting one's mind into health and exercising it and training it to think properly, is only the beginning of the task before the awakening Open Conspirator. He has not only to think clearly, but he has to see that his mind is equipped with the proper general ideas to form a true framework for his everyday judgments and decisions.

It was the Great War first brought home to me how ignorant I was, and how ill-finished and untidy my mind, about the most important things of life. That disastrous waste of life, material and happiness, since it was practically world wide, was manifestly the outcome of the processes that constitute the bulk of history, and yet I found I did not know – and nobody else seemed to know – history in such a fashion as to be able to explain how the Great War came about or what ought to come out of it. "Versailles," we all seem to be agreed nowadays, was silly, but how could Versailles be anything else than what it was in view of the imperfect, lopsided, historical knowledge and the consequent suspicion, emotion, and prejudice of those who assembled there. They did not know any better than the rest of us what the war was, and so how could they know what the peace ought to be? I perceived that I was in the same case with everyone else, and I set myself first of all for my own guidance to make a summary of all history and get some sort of map to more serviceable conclusions about the political state of mankind. This summary I made was *The Outline of History*, a shameless compilation and arrangement of the main facts of the world story, written without a touch of art or elegance, written indeed in a considerable hurry and excitement, and its sale, which is now in the third million, showed how much I had in common with a great dispersed crowd of ordinary people, all wanting to know, all disgusted with the patriotic, litigious twaddling gossipy stuff given them as history by their schoolmasters and schoolmistresses which had led them into the disaster of the war.

The Outline of History is not a whole history of life. Its main theme is the growth of human intercommunication and human communities and their rulers and conflicts, the story of how and why the myriads of little tribal systems of ten thousand years ago have fought and coalesced into the sixty- or seventy-odd governments of to-day and are now straining and labouring in the grip of forces that must presently accomplish their final unison. And even as I completed *The Outline*, I realized that there remained outside its scope wider and more fundamental, and closer, more immediate fields of knowledge which I still had to get in order for my own practical ends and the ends of like-minded people who wanted to use their lives effectively, if my existence was to escape futility.

I realized that I did not know enough about the life in my body and its relations to the world of life and matter outside it to come to proper decisions about a number of urgent matters – from race conflicts, birth control, and my private life, to the public control of health and the conservation of natural resources. And also, I found, I was astonishingly ignorant about the everyday business of life, the how and why of the miner who provided the coal to cook my dinner, and the banker who took my money in return for a cheque-book, and the shopkeeper from whom I bought things, and the policeman who kept the streets in order for me. Yet I was voting for laws affecting my relations with these people, paying them directly or indirectly, airing my ignorant opinions about them, and generally contributing by my behaviour to sustain and affect their lives.

So with the aid and direction of two very competent biologists I set to work to get out as plain and clear a statement as possible of what was known about the sources and nature of life and the relation of species to individuals and to other species, and the processes of consciousness and thought. This I published as *The Science of Life*. And while this was going on I set myself to the task of making a review of all human activities in relation to each other, the work of people and the needs of people, cultivation, manufacture, trade, direction, government, and all. This was the most difficult part of this attempt to get a rational account of the modern world, and it called for the help and counsel of a great variety of people. I had to ask and find some general answer to the question, "What are the nineteen hundred-odd million human beings who are alive to-day doing, and how and why are they doing it?" It was, in fact, an outline of economic, social, and political science, but since, after *The Outline of History*, the word "outline" has been a good deal cheapened by various enterprising publishers, I have called it, *The Work, Wealth, and Happiness of Mankind*.

Now, I find, by getting these three correlated compilations into existence, I have at last, in however rough a fashion, brought together a complete system of ideas upon which an Open Conspirator can go. Before anyone could hope to get on to anything like a practical working directive answer to "What are we to do with our lives?" it was necessary to know what our lives were – *The Science of Life*; what had led up to their present pattern – *The Outline of History*; and this third book, to tell what we were actually doing and supposed to be doing with our working lives, day by day, at the present time. By the time I was through with these books I felt I had really something sound and comprehensive to go upon, an "ideology," as people say, on which it was possible to think of building a new world without fundamental surprises, and, moreover, that I had got my mind stripped down and cleaned of many illusions and bad habits, so that it could handle life with an assurance it had never known before.

There is nothing marvellous about these compilations of mine. Any steady writer of average intelligence with the same will and the same resources, who could devote about nine or ten years to the task and get the proper sort of help, could have made them. It can be done, it is no doubt being done, all over again by other people, for themselves and perhaps for others, much more beautifully and adequately. But to get that amount of vision and knowledge, to achieve that general arrangement and under standing, was a necessary condition that had to be satisfied before any answer to the question, "What are we to do with our lives?" could even be attempted, and before one could become in any effective way an Open Conspirator.

There is nothing indispensable even now, I repeat, about these three particular books. I know about them and refer to them because I put them together myself and so they are handy for me to explain myself. But most of what they contain can be extracted from any good encyclopaedia. Any number of people have made similar outlines of history for themselves, have read widely, grasped the leading principles of biology and grappled with the current literature of business science and do not in the least need my particular summary. So far as history and biology are concerned there are parallel books, that are as good and serviceable. Van Loon's books for example. Yet even for highly-educated people these summaries may be useful in bringing things known with different degrees of thoroughness, into a general scheme. They correlate, and they fill up gaps. Between them they cover the ground; and in some fashion that ground has to be covered before the mind of a modern citizen is prepared to tackle the problems that confront it. Otherwise he is an incapable citizen, he does not know where he is and where the world is, and if he is rich or influential he may be a very dangerous citizen indeed. Presently there will be far better compilations to meet this need, or perhaps the gist of all the three divisions of knowledge, concentrated and made more lucid and attractive, may be available as the intellectual frame of modern education throughout the world, as a "General Account of Life" that should be given to everyone.

But certainly no one can possibly set about living properly and satisfactorily unless he knows what he is, where he is, and how he stands to the people and things about him.

IV

THE REVOLUTION IN EDUCATION

Some sort of reckoning therefore between people awakened to the new world that dawns about us and the schools, colleges, and machinery of formal education is overdue. As a body the educated are getting nothing like that Account of Life which is needed to direct our conduct in this modern world.

It is the crowning absurdity in the world to-day that these institutions should go through a solemn parade of preparing the new generation for life and that then, afterwards, a minority of their victims, finding this preparation has left them almost totally unprepared, should have of their own accord to struggle out of our world heap of starved and distorted minds to some sort of real education. The world cannot be run by such a minority of escaped and re-educated minds alone, with all the rest of the heap against them. Our necessities demand the intelligence and services of everyone who can be trained to give them. The new world demands new schools, therefore, to give everyone a sound and thorough mental training and equip everyone with clear ideas about history, about life, and about political and economic relationships instead of the rubbishy head-content at present prevalent. The old-world teachers and schools have to be reformed or replaced. A vigorous educational reform movement arises as a natural and necessary expression of the awakening Open Conspirator. A revolution in education is the most imperative and fundamental part of the adaptation of life to its new conditions.

These various compendia of knowledge constituting a Modern Account of Life, on which we have laid stress in the previous section, these supplements to teaching, which are now produced and read outside the established formal educational world and in the teeth of its manifest hostility, arise because of the backwardness of that world, and as that world yields slowly but surely to the pressure of the new spirit, so they will permeate and replace its text-books and disappear as a separate class of book. The education these new dangerous times in which we are now living demands, must start right, from the beginning and there must be nothing to replace and nothing to relearn in it. Before we can talk politics, finance, business, or morals, we must see that we have got the right mental habits and the right foundation of realized facts. There is nothing much to be done with our lives until we have seen to that.

V

RELIGION IN THE NEW WORLD

"Yes," objects a reader, "but does not our religion tell us what we are to do with our lives?"

We have to bring religion, as a fundamental matter, into this discussion. From our present point of view religion is that central essential part of education which determines conduct. Religion certainly should tell us what to do with our lives. But in the vast stir and occasions of modern life, so much of what we call religion remains irrelevant or dumb. Religion does not seem to "join on" to the main parts of the general problem of living. It has lost touch.

Let us try and bring this problem of the Open Conspiracy to meet and make the new world, into relation with the traditions of religion. The clear-minded Open Conspirator who has got his modern ideology, his lucidly arranged account of the universe in order, is obliged to believe that only by giving his life to the great processes of social reconstruction, and shaping his conduct with reference to that, can he do well with his life. But that merely launches him into the most subtle and unending of struggles, the struggle against the incessant gravitation of our interests to ourselves. He has to live the broad life and escape from the close narrow life. We all try to attain the dignity and happiness of magnanimity and escape from the tormenting urgencies of personal desire. In the past that struggle has generally assumed the form of a religious struggle. Religion is the antagonist of self.

In their completeness, in the life that was professionally *religious*, religions have always demanded great subordinations of self. Therein lay their creative force. They demanded devotion and gave reasons for that demand. They disentangled the will from the egotistical preoccupations – often very completely. There is no such thing as a self-contained religion, a private religious solo. Certain forms of Protestantism and some mystical types come near to making religion a secluded duet between the individual and his divinity, but here that may be regarded as a perversion of the religious impulse. Just as the normal sexual complex excites and stirs the individual out of his egotism to serve the ends of the race, so the normal religious process takes the individual out of his egotism for the service of the community. It is not a bargain, a "social contract," between the individual and the community; it is a subordination of both the existing individual and the existing community in relation to something, a divinity, a divine order, a standard, a righteousness, more important than either. What is called in the phraseology of certain religions "conviction of sin" and "the flight from the City of Destruction" are familiar instances of this reference of the self-centred individual and the current social life to something far better than either the one or the other.

This is the third element in the religious relationship, a hope, a promise, an objective which turns the convert not only from himself but from the "world,"as it is, towards better things. First comes self-disregard, then service, and then this reconstructive creative urgency.

For the finer sort of mind this aspect of religion seems always to have been its primary attraction. One has to remember that there is a real will for religion scattered throughout mankind – a real desire to get away from self. Religion has never pursued its distinctive votaries; they have come to meet it. The desire to give oneself to greater ends than the everyday life affords, and to give oneself freely, is clearly dominant in that minority, and traceable in an incalculable proportion of the majority.

But hitherto religion has never been presented *simply* as a devotion to a universal cause. The devotion has always been in it, but it has been complicated by other considerations. The leaders in every great religious movement have considered it necessary that it should explain itself in the form of history and a cosmogony. It has been felt necessary to say *Why?* and *To what end?* Every religion therefore has had to adopt the physical conceptions, and usually also to assume many of the moral and social values, current at the time of its foundation. It could not transcend the philosophical phrases and attitudes that seemed then to supply the natural frame for a faith, nor draw upon anything beyond the store of scientific knowledge of its time. In this lurked the seeds of the ultimate decay and supersession of every successive religion.

But as the idea of continual change, going farther and farther from existing realities and never returning to them, is a new one, as nobody until very recently has grasped the fact that the knowledge of to-day is the ignorance of to-morrow, each fresh development of religion in the world so far has been proclaimed in perfect good faith as the culminating and final truth.

This finality of statement has considerable immediate practical value. The suggestion of the possibility of further restatement is an unsettling suggestion; it undermines conviction and breaks the ranks of the believers, because there are enormous variations in the capacities of men to recognize the same spirit under a changing shape. Those variations cause endless difficulties to-day. While some intelligences can recognize the same God under a variety of names and symbols without any severe strain, others cannot even detect the most contrasted Gods one from the other, provided they wear the same mask and title. It appears a perfectly natural and reasonable thing to many minds to restate religion now in terms of biological and psychological necessity, while to others any variation whatever in the phrasing of the faith seems to be nothing less than atheistical misrepresentations of the most damnable kind. For these latter God, a God still anthropomorphic enough to have a will and purpose, to display preferences and reciprocate emotions, to be indeed a person, must be retained until the end of time. For others, God can be thought of as a Great First Cause, as impersonal and inhuman as atomic structure.

It is because of the historical and philosophical commitments they have undertaken, and because of concessions made to common human weaknesses in regard to such once apparently minor but now vital moral issues as property, mental activity, and public veracity – rather than of any inadequacy in their adaptation to psychological needs – that the present wide discredit of organized religions has come about. They no longer seem even roughly truthful upon issues of fact, and they give no imperatives over large fields of conduct in which perplexity is prevalent. People will say, "I could be perfectly happy leading the life of a Catholic devotee if only I could believe." But most of the framework of religious explanation upon which that life is sustained is too old-fashioned and too irrelevant to admit of that thoroughness of belief which is necessary for the devotion of intelligent people

Great ingenuity has been shown by modern writers and thinkers in the adaptation of venerated religious expressions to new ideas. *Peccavi.* Have I not written of the creative will in humanity as "God the Invisible King" and presented it in the figure of a youthful and adventurous finite god?

The word "God" is in most minds so associated with the concept of religion that it is abandoned only with the greatest reluctance. The word remains, though the idea is continually attenuated. Respect for Him demands that He should have no limitations. He is pushed farther and farther from actuality, therefore, and His definition becomes increasingly a bundle of negations, until at last, in His role of The Absolute, He becomes an entirely negative expression. While we can speak of good, say some, we can speak of God. God is the possibility of goodness, the good side of things. If phrases in which the name of God is used are to be abandoned, they argue, religion will be left speechless before many occasions.

Certainly there is something beyond the individual that is and the world that is; on that we have already insisted as a characteristic of all religions; that persuasion is the essence of faith and the key to courage. But whether that is to be considered, even after the most strenuous exercises in personification, as a greater person or a comprehensive person, is another matter. Personality is the last vestige of anthropomorphism. The modern urge to a precise veracity is against such concessions to traditional expression.

On the other hand there is in many fine religious minds a desire amounting almost to a necessity for an object of devotion so individualized as to be capable at least of a receptive consciousness even if no definite response is conceded. One type of mind can accept a reality in itself which another must project and dramatize before it can comprehend it and react to it. The human soul is an intricate thing which will not endure elucidation when that passes beyond a certain degree of harshness and roughness. The human spirit has learnt love, devotion, obedience and humility in relation to other personalities, and with difficulty it takes the final step to a transcendent subordination, from which the last shred of personality has been stripped.

In matters not immediately material, language has to work by metaphors, and though every metaphor carries its own peculiar risks of confusion, we cannot do without them. Great intellectual tolerance is necessary, therefore – a cultivated disposition to translate and retranslate from one metaphysical or emotional idiom to another – if there is not to be a deplorable wastage of moral force in our world. Just now I wrote *Peccavi* because I had written *God the Invisible King*, but after all I do not think it was so much a sin to use that phrase, God the Invisible King, as an error in expression. If there is no sympathetic personal leader outside us, there is at least in us the attitude we should adopt towards a sympathetic personal leader.

Three profound differences between the new mental dispositions of the present time and those of preceding ages have to be realized if current developments of the religious impulse are to be seen in their correct relationship to the religious life of the past. There has been a great advance in the analysis of psychic processes and the courage with which men have probed into the origins of human thought and feeling. Following upon the biological advances that have made us recognize fish and amphibian in the bodily structure of man, have come these parallel developments in which we see elemental fear and lust and self-love moulded, modified, and exalted, under the stress of social progress, into intricate human motives. Our conception of sin and our treatment of sin have been profoundly modified by this analysis. Our former sins are seen as ignorances, inadequacies and bad habits, and the moral conflict is robbed of three-fourths of its ego-centred melodramatic quality. We are no longer moved to be less wicked; we are moved to organize our conditioned reflexes and lead a life less fragmentary and silly.

Secondly, the conception of individuality has been influenced and relaxed by biological thought, so that we do not think so readily of the individual *contra mundum* as our fathers did. We begin to realize that we are egotists by misapprehension. Nature cheats the self to serve the purposes of the species by filling it with wants that war against its private interests. As our eyes are opened to these things, we see ourselves as beings greater or less than the definitive self. Man's soul is no longer his own. It is, he discovers, part of a greater being which lived before he was born and will survive him. The idea of a survival of the definite individual with all the accidents and idiosyncrasies of his temporal nature upon him dissolves to nothing in this new view of immortality.

The third of the main contrasts between modern and former thought which have rendered the general shapes of established religion old-fashioned and unserviceable is a reorientation of current ideas about time. The powerful disposition of the human mind to explain everything as the inevitable unfolding of a past event which, so to speak, sweeps the future helplessly before it, has been checked by a mass of subtle criticisms. The conception of progress as a broadening and increasing purpose, a conception which is taking hold of the human imagination more and more firmly, turns religious life towards the future. We think no longer of submission to the irrevocable decrees of absolute dominion, but of participation in an adventure on behalf of a power that gains strength and establishes itself. The history of our world, which has been unfolded to us by science, runs counter to all the histories on which religions have been based. There was no Creation in the past, we begin to realize, but eternally there is creation; there was no Fall to account for the conflict of good and evil, but a stormy ascent. Life as we know it is a mere beginning.

It seems unavoidable that if religion is to develop unifying and directive power in the present confusion of human affairs it must adapt itself to this forward-looking, individuality-analyzing turn of mind; it must divest itself of its sacred histories, its gross preoccupations, its posthumous prolongation of personal ends. *The desire for service, for subordination, for permanent effect, for an escape from the distressful pettiness and mortality of the individual life, is the undying element in every religious system.*

The time has come to strip religion right down to that, to strip it for greater tasks than it has ever faced before. The histories and symbols that served our fathers encumber and divide us. Sacraments and rituals harbour disputes and waste our scanty emotions. *The explanation of why things are is an unnecessary effort in religion.* The essential fact in religion is the desire for religion and not how it came about. If you do not want religion, no persuasions, no convictions about your place in the universe can give it to you. The first sentence in the modern creed must be, not "I believe," but "I give myself."

To what? And how? To these questions we will now address ourselves.

66

VI

MODERN RELIGION IS OBJECTIVE

To give oneself religiously is a continuing operation expressed in a series of acts. It can be nothing else. You cannot dedicate yourself and then go away to live just as you have lived before. It is a poor travesty of religion that does not produce an essential change in the life which embraces it. But in the established and older religions of our race, this change of conduct has involved much self-abasement merely to the God or Gods, or much self-mortification merely with a view to the moral perfecting of self. Christian devotion, for example, in these early stages, before the hermit life gave place to organized monastic life, did not to any extent direct itself to service except the spiritual service of other human beings. But as Christianity became a definite social organizing force, it took on a great series of healing, comforting, helping, and educational activities.

The modern tendency has been and is all in the direction of minimizing what one might call self-centred devotion and self-subjugation, and of expanding and developing external service. The idea of inner perfectibility dwindles with the diminishing importance attached to individuality. We cease to think of mortifying or exalting or perfecting ourselves and seek to lose ourselves in a greater life. We think less and less of "conquering" self and more and more of escaping from self. If we attempt to perfect ourselves in any respect it is only as a soldier sharpens and polishes an essential weapon.

Our quickened apprehension of continuing change, our broader and fuller vision of the history of life, disabuse our minds of many limitations set to the imaginations of our predecessors. Much that they saw as fixed and determinate, we see as transitory and controllable. They saw life fixed in its species and subjected to irrevocable laws. We see life struggling insecurely but with a gathering successfulness for freedom and power against restriction and death. We see life coming at last to our tragic and hopeful human level. Unprecedented possibilities, mighty problems, we realize, confront mankind to-day. They frame our existences. The practical aspect, the material form, the embodiment of the modernized religious impulse is the direction of the whole life to the solution of these problems and the realization of their possibilities. The alternative before man now is either magnificence of spirit and magnificence of achievement, or disaster.

The modern religious life, like all forms of religious life, must needs have its own subtle and deep inner activities, its meditations, its self-confrontations, its phases of stress and search and appeal, its serene and prayerful moods, but these inward aspects do not come into the scope of this present inquiry, which is concerned entirely with the outward shape, the direction, and the organization of modern religious effort, with the question of what, given religious devotion, we have to do and how that has to be done.

Now, in the new and greater universe to which we are awakening, its immense possibilities furnish an entirely new frame and setting for the moral life. In the fixed and limited outlook of the past, practical good works took the form mainly of palliative measures against evils that were conceived of as incurable; the religious community nursed the sick, fed the hungry, provided sanctuary for the fugitive, pleaded with the powerful for mercy. It did not dream of preventing sickness, famine, or tyranny. Other-worldliness was its ready refuge from the invincible evil and confusion of the existing scheme of things.

But it is possible now to imagine an order in human affairs from which these evils have been largely or entirely eliminated. More and more people are coming to realize that such an order is a material possibility. And with the realization that this is a material possibility, we can no longer be content with a field of "good deeds" and right action restricted to palliative and consolatory activities. Such things are merely "first aid." The religious mind grows bolder than it has ever been before. It pushes through the curtain it once imagined was a barrier. It apprehends its larger obligations. The way in which our activities conduce to the realization of that conceivable better order in human affairs, becomes the new criterion of conduct. Other-worldliness has become unnecessary.

The realization of this possible better order brings us at once to certain definite lines of conduct. We have to make an end to war, and to make an end to war we must be cosmopolitan in our politics. It is impossible for any clearheaded person to suppose that the ever more destructive stupidities of war can be eliminated from human affairs until some common political control dominates the earth, and unless certain pressures due to the growth of population, due to the enlarging scope of economic operations or due to conflicting standards and traditions of life, are disposed of.

To avoid the positive evils of war and to attain the new levels of prosperity and power that now come into view, an effective world control, not merely of armed force, but of the production and main movements of staple commodities and the drift and expansion of population is required. It is absurd to dream of peace and world-wide progress without that much control. These things assured, the abilities and energies of a greatly increased proportion of human beings could be diverted to the happy activities of scientific research and creative work, with an ever-increasing release and enlargement of human possibility. On the political side it is plain that our lives must be given to the advancement of that union.

Such a forward stride in human life, the first stride in a mighty continuing advance, an advance to which no limit appears, is now not simply materially possible. It is urgent. The opportunity is plain before mankind. It is the alternative to social decay. But there is no certainty, no material necessity, that it should ever be taken. It will not be taken by mankind inadvertently. It can only be taken through such an organization of will and energy to take it as this world has never seen before.

These are the new imperatives that unfold themselves before the more alert minds of our generation. They will presently become the general mental background, as the modern interpretations of the history of life and of the material and mental possibilities about us establish themselves. Evil political, social, and economic usages and arrangements may seem obdurate and huge, but they are neither permanent nor uncontrollable. They can be controlled, however, only by an effort more powerful and determined than the instincts and inertias that sustain them. Religion, modern and disillusioned, has for its outward task to set itself to the control and direction of political, social, and economic life. If it does not do that, then it is no more than a drug for easing discomfort, "the opium of the peoples."

Can religion, or can it not, synthesize the needed effort to lift mankind out of our present disorders, dangers, baseness, frustrations, and futilities to a phase of relative security, accumulating knowledge, systematic and continuing growth in power and the widespread, deep happiness of hopeful and increasing life?

Our answer here is that the religious spirit, in the light of modern knowledge, can do this thing, and our subject now is to enquire what are the necessary opening stages in the synthesis of that effort. We write, from this point onward, for those who believe that it can, and who do already grasp the implications of world history and contemporary scientific achievement.

VII

What Mankind Has To Do

BEFORE we can consider the forms and methods of attacking this inevitable task of reconstruction it will be well to draw the main lines and to attempt some measure of the magnitude of that task. What are the new forms that it is thus proposed to impose upon human life, and how are they to be evolved from or imposed upon the current forms ? And against what passive and active resistances has this to be done ?

There can be no pause for replacement in the affairs of life. Day must follow day, and the common activities continue. The new world as a going concern must arise out of the old as a going concern.

Now the most comprehensive conception of this new world is of one politically, socially, and economically unified. Within that frame fall all the other ideas of our progressive ambition. To this end we set our faces and seek to direct our lives. Many there are at present who apprehend it as a possibility but do not *dare*, it seems, to desire it, because of the enormous difficulties that intervene, and because they see as yet no intimations of a way through or round these difficulties. They do not see a way of escape from the patchwork of governments that grips them and divides mankind. The great majority of human beings have still to see the human adventure as one whole; they are obsessed by the air of permanence and finality in established things; they accept current reality as ultimate reality. As the saying goes, they take the world as they find it.

But here we are writing for the modern-minded, and for them it is impossible to think of the world as secure and satisfactory until there exists a single world commonweal, preventing war and controlling those moral, biological, and economic forces and wastages that would otherwise lead to wars. And controlling them in the sense that science and man's realization and control of his powers and possibilities continually increase.

Let us make clear what sort of government we are trying to substitute for the patchwork of to-day. It will be a new sort of direction with a new psychology. The method of direction of such a world commonweal is not likely to imitate the methods of existing sovereign states. It will be some thing new and altogether different.

This point is not yet generally realized. It is too often assumed that the world commonweal will be, as it were, just the one heir and survivor of existing states, and that it will be a sort of megatherium of the same form and anatomy as its predecessors.

But a little reflection will show that this is a mistake. Existing states are primarily militant states, and a world state cannot be militant. There will be little need for president or king to lead the marshalled hosts of humanity, for where there is no war there is no need of any leader to lead hosts any where, and in a polyglot world a parliament of mankind or any sort of council that meets and talks is an inconceivable instrument of government. The voice will cease to be a suitable vehicle. World government, like scientific process, will be conducted by statement, criticism, and publication that will be capable of efficient translation.

The fundamental organization of contemporary states is plainly still military, and that is exactly what a world organization cannot be. Flags, uniforms, national anthems, patriotism sedulously cultivated in church and school, the brag, blare, and bluster of our competing sovereignties, belong to the phase of development the Open Conspiracy will supersede. We have to get clear of that clutter. The reasonable desire of all of us is that we should have the collective affairs of the world managed by suitably equipped groups of the most interested, intelligent, and devoted people, and that their activities should be subjected to a free, open, watchful criticism, restrained from making spasmodic interruptions but powerful enough to modify or supersede without haste or delay whatever is weakening or unsatisfactory in the general direction.

A number of readers will be disposed to say that this is a very vague, undefined, and complicated conception of world government. But indeed it is a simplification. Not only are the present governments of the world a fragmentary competitive confusion, but none of them is as simple as it appears. They seem to be simple because they have formal heads and definite forms, councils, voting assemblies, and so forth, for arriving at decisions. But the formal heads, the kings, presidents, and so forth, are really not the directive heads. They are merely the figure heads. They do not decide. They merely make gestures of potent and dignified acquiescence when decisions are put to them. They are complicating shams. Nor do the councils and assemblies really decide. They record, often very imperfectly and exasperatingly, the accumulating purpose of outer forces. These outer really directive forces are no doubt very intricate in their operation; they depend finally on religious and educational forms and upon waves of gregarious feeling, but it does not in the least simplify the process of collective human activity to pretend that it is simple and to set up symbols and dummies in the guise of rulers and dictators to embody that pretence. To recognize the incurable intricacy of collective action is a mental simplification; to remain satisfied with the pretensions of existing governmental institutions, and to bring in all the problems of their procedure and interaction is to complicate the question.

71

The present rudimentary development of collective psychology obliges us to be vague and provisional about the way in which the collective mind may best define its will for the purpose of administrative action. We may know that a thing is possible and still be unable to do it as yet, just as we knew that aviation was possible in 1900. Some method of decision there must certainly be and a definite administrative machinery. But it may turn out to be a much slighter, less elaborate organization than a consideration of existing methods might lead us to imagine. It may never become one single interlocking administrative system. We may have systems of world control rather than a single world state. The practical regulations, enforcements, and officials needed to keep the world in good health, for example, may be only very loosely related to the system of controls that will maintain its communications in a state of efficiency. Enforcement and legal decisions, as we know them now, may be found to be enormously and needlessly cumbrous by our descendants. As the reasonableness of a thing is made plain, the need for its enforcement is diminished, and the necessity for litigation disappears.

The Open Conspiracy, the world movement for the supersession or enlargement or fusion of existing political, economic, and social institutions must necessarily, as it grows, draw closer and closer to questions of practical control. It is likely in its growth to incorporate many active public servants and many industrial and financial leaders and directors. It may also assimilate great masses of intelligent workers. As its activities spread it will work out a whole system of special methods of co-operation. As it grows, and by growing, it will learn the business of general direction and how to develop its critical function. A lucid, dispassionate, and immanent criticism is the primary necessity, the living spirit of a world civilization. The Open Conspiracy is essentially such a criticism, and the carrying out of such a criticism into working reality is the task of the Open Conspiracy. It will by its very nature be aiming not so much to set up a world direction as to become itself a world direction, and the educational and militant forms of its opening phase will evoke, step by step, as experience is gained and power and responsibility acquired, forms of administration and research and correlation.

The differences in nature and function between the world controls of the future and the state governments of the present age which we have just pointed out favours a hope that the Open Conspiracy may come to its own in many cases rather by the fading out of these state governments through the inhibition and paralysis of their destructive militant and competitive activities than by a direct conflict to overthrow them. As new world controls develop, it becomes the supreme business of the Open Conspiracy to keep them world wide and impartial, to save them by an incessant critical educational and propagandist activity from entanglement with the old traditional rivalries and feuds of states and nations. It is quite possible that such world controls should be able to develop independently, but it is highly probable, on the other hand, that they will continue to be entangled as they are to-day, and that they will need to be disengaged with a struggle. We repeat, the new directive organizations of men's affairs will not be of the same nature as old-fashioned governments. They will be in their nature biological, financial, and generally economic, and the old governments were primarily nothing of the sort. Their directive force will be (1) an effective criticism having the quality of science, and (2) the growing will in men to have things right. The directive force of the older governments was the uncriticized fantasies and willfulness of an individual, a class, a tribe, or a majority.

The modernization of the religious impulse leads us straight to this effort for the establishment of the world state as a duty, and the close consideration of the necessary organization of that effort will bring the reader to the conclusion that a movement aiming at the establishment of a world directorate, however restricted that movement may be at first in numbers and power, must either contemplate the prospect of itself developing into a world directorate, and by the digestion and assimilation of superseded factors into an entire modern world community, or admit from the outset the futility, the spare-time amateurishness, of its gestures.

VIII

Broad Characteristics Of A Scientific World Commonweal

Continuing our examination of the practical task before the modern mind, we may next note the main lines of contemporary aspiration within this comprehensive outline of a world commonweal. Any sort of unification of human affairs will not serve the ends we seek. We aim at a particular sort of unification; a world Caesar is hardly better from the progressive viewpoint than world chaos; the unity we seek must mean a world-wide liberation of thought, experiment and creative effort.

A successful Open Conspiracy merely to seize governments and wield and retain world power would be at best only the empty frame of success. It might be the exact reverse of success. Release from the threat of war and from the waste of international economic conflicts is a poor release if it demands as its price the loss of all other liberties.

It is because we desire a unification of human direction, not simply for the sake of unity, but as a means of release to happiness and power, that it is necessary, at any cost – in delay, in loss of effective force, in strategic or tactical disadvantage – that the light of free, abundant criticism should play upon that direction and upon the movements and unifying organizations leading to the establishment of that unifying direction.

Man is an imperfect animal and never quite trustworthy in the dark. Neither morally nor intellectually is he safe from lapses. Most of us who are past our first youth know how little we can trust ourselves and are glad to have our activities checked and guarded by a sense of helpful inspection. It is for this reason that a movement to realize the conceivable better state of the world must deny itself the advantages of secret methods or tactical insincerities. It must leave that to its adversaries. We must declare our end plainly from the outset and risk no misunderstandings of our procedure.

The Open Conspiracy against the traditional and now cramping and dangerous institutions of the world must be an Open Conspiracy and cannot remain righteous otherwise. It is lost if it goes underground. Every step to world unity must be taken in the daylight with the understanding sympathy of as many people as possible, or the sort of unity that will be won will be found to be scarcely worth the winning. The essential task would have to be recommenced again within the mere frame of unity thus attained.

This candid attempt to take possession of the whole world, this Open Conspiracy of ours, must be made in the name of and for the sake of science and creative activity. Its aim is to release science and creative ability and every stage in the struggle must be watched and criticized, lest there be any sacrifice of these ends to the exigencies of conflict.

The security of creative progress and creative activity implies a competent regulation of the economic life in the collective interest. There must be food, shelter and leisure for all. The fundamental needs of the animal life must be assured before human life can have free play. Man does not live by bread alone; he eats that he may learn and adventure creatively, but unless he eats he cannot adventure. His life is primarily economic, as a house is primarily a foundation, and economic justice and efficiency must underlie all other activities; but to judge human society and organize political and social activities entirely on economic grounds is to forget the objectives of life's campaign in a preoccupation with supply.

It is true that man, like the animal world in general from which he has risen, is the creature of a struggle for sustenance, but unlike the animals, man can resort to methods of escape from that competitive pressure upon the means of subsistence, which has been the lot of every other animal species. He can restrain the increase in his numbers, and he seems capable of still quite undefined expansions of his productivity per head of population. He can escape therefore from the struggle for subsistence altogether with a surplus of energy such as no other kind of animal species has ever possessed. Intelligent control of population is a possibility which puts man outside competitive processes that have hitherto ruled the modification of species, and he can be released from these processes in no other way.

There is a clear hope that, later, directed breeding will come within his scope, but that goes beyond his present range of practical achievement, and we need not discuss it further here. Suffice it for us here that the world community of our desires, the organized world community conducting and ensuring its own progress, requires a deliberate collective control of population as a primary condition.

There is no strong instinctive desire for multitudinous offspring, as such, in the feminine make-up. The reproductive impulses operate indirectly. Nature ensures a pressure of population through passions and instincts that, given sufficient knowledge, intelligence, and freedom on the part of women, can be satisfactorily gratified and tranquillized, if need be, without the production of numerous children. Very slight adjustments in social and economic arrangements will, in a world of clear available knowledge and straightforward practice in these matters, supply sufficient inducement or discouragement to affect the general birth rate or the birth rate of specific types as the directive sense of the community may consider desirable. So long as the majority of human beings are begotten involuntarily in lust and ignorance, so long does man remain like any other animal under the moulding pressure of competition for subsistence. Social and political processes change entirely in their character when we recognize the possibility and practicability of this fundamental revolution in human biology.

In a world so relieved, the production of staple necessities presents a series of problems altogether less distressful than those of the present scramble for possessions and self-indulgence on the part of the successful, and for work and a bare living on the part of the masses. With the increase of population unrestrained, there was, as the end of the economic process, no practical alternative to a multitudinous equality at the level of bare subsistence, except through such an inequality of economic arrangements as allowed a minority to maintain a higher standard of life by withholding whatever surplus of production it could grasp, from consumption in mere proletarian breeding. In the past and at present, what is called the capitalist system, that is to say the unsystematic exploitation of production by private owners under the protection of the law, has, on the whole, in spite of much waste and conflict, worked beneficially by checking that gravitation to a universal low-grade consumption which would have been the inevitable outcome of a socialism oblivious of biological processes. With effective restraint upon the increase of population, however, entirely new possibilities open out before mankind.

The besetting vice of economic science, orthodox and unorthodox alike, has been the vice of beginning in the air, with current practice and current convictions, with questions of wages, prices, values, and possession, when the profounder issues of human association are really not to be found at all on these levels. The primary issues of human association are biological and psychological, and the essentials of economics are problems in applied physics and chemistry. The first thing we should examine is what we want to do with natural resources, and the next, how to get men to do what has to be done as pleasurably and effectively as possible. Then we should have a standard by which to judge the methods of to-day.

But the academic economists, and still more so Marx and his followers, refuse to deal with these fundamentals, and, with a stupid pose of sound practical wisdom, insist on opening up their case with an uncritical acceptance of the common antagonism of employers and employed and a long rigmarole about profits and wages. Ownership and expropriated labour are only one set of many possible sets of economic method.

The economists, however, will attend seriously only to the current set; the rest they ignore; and the Marxists, with their uncontrollable disposition to use nicknames in the place of judgments, condemn all others as "Utopian" – a word as final in its dismissal from the minds of the elect as that other pet counter in the Communist substitute for thought, "Bourgeois." If they can persuade themselves that an idea or a statement is "Utopian" or "Bourgeois," it does not seem to matter in the least to them whether it is right or wrong. It is disposed of. Just as in genteeler circles anything is disposed of that can be labelled "atheistical," "subversive" or "disloyal."

If a century and a half ago the world had submitted its problems of transport to the economists, they would have put aside, with as little wasted breath and ink as possible, all talk about railways, motorcars, steamships, and aeroplanes, and, with a fine sense of extravagance rebuked, set themselves to long neuralgic dissertations, disputations, and treatises upon highroads and the methods of connecting them, turnpike gates, canals, the influence of lock fees on bargemen, tidal landing places, anchorages, surplus carrying capacity, carriers, caravans, hand-barrows, and the pedestrianariat. There would have been a rapid and easy differentiation in feeling and requirements between the horse-owning minority and the walking majority; the wrongs of the latter would have tortured the mind of every philosopher who could not ride, and been minimized by every philosopher who could; and there would have been a broad rift between the narrow-footpath school, the no-footpath school, and the school which would look forward to a time when every horse would have to be led along one universal footpath under the dictatorship of the pedestrianariat All with the profoundest gravity and dignity. These things, footpaths and roads and canals with their traffic, were "real," and "Utopian" projects for getting along at thirty or forty miles an hour or more uphill and against wind and tide, let alone the still more incredible suggestion of air transport, would have been smiled and sneered out of court. Life went about on its legs, with a certain assistance from wheels, or floated, rowed and was blown about on water; so it had been – and so it would always be.

The psychology of economic co-operation is still only dawning, and so the economists and the doctrinaire socialists have had the freest range for pedantry and authoritative pomp. For a hundred years they have argued and argued about "rent," about " surplus value," and so on, and have produced a literature ten thousand times as bulky, dreary, and foolish as the worst outpourings of the mediaeval schoolmen.

But as soon as this time-honoured preoccupation with the allotment of the shares of originators, organizers, workers, owners of material, credit dealers, and tax collectors in the total product, ceases to be dealt with as the primary question in economics; as soon as we liberate our minds from a preoccupation which from the outset necessarily makes that science a squabble rather than a science, and begin our attack upon the subject with a survey of the machinery and other productive material required in order that the staple needs of mankind should be satisfied, if we go on from that to consider the way in which all this material and machinery can be worked and the product distributed with the least labour and the greatest possible satisfaction, we shift our treatment of economic questions towards standards by which all current methods of exploitation, employment, and finance can be judged rather than wrangled over. We can dismiss the question of the claims of this sort of participant or that, for later and subordinate consideration, and view each variety of human assistance in the general effort entirely from the standpoint of what makes that assistance least onerous and most effective.

The germs of such really scientific economics exist already in the study of industrial organization and industrial psychology. As the science of industrial psychology in particular develops, we shall find all this discussion of ownership, profit, wages, finance, and accumulation, which has been treated hitherto as the primary issues of economics, falling into place under the larger enquiry of what conventions in these matters, what system of money and what conceptions of property, yield the greatest stimulus and the least friction in that world-wide system of co-operation which must constitute the general economic basis to the activities of a unified mankind.

Manifestly the supreme direction of the complex of human economic activities in such a world must centre upon a bureau of information and advice, which will take account of all the resources of the planet, estimate current needs, apportion productive activities and control distribution. The topographical and geological surveys of modern civilized communities, their government maps, their periodic issue of agricultural and industrial statistics, are the first crude and unco-ordinated beginnings of such an economic world intelligence. In the propaganda work of David Lubin, a pioneer whom mankind must not forget, and in his International Institute of Agriculture in Rome, there were the beginnings of an impartial review month by month and year by year of world production, world needs and world transport. Such a great central organization of economic science would necessarily produce direction; it would indicate what had best be done here, there, and everywhere, solve general tangles, examine, approve and initiate fresh methods and arrange the transitional process from old to new. It would not be an organization of will, imposing its will upon a reluctant or recalcitrant race; it would be a direction, just as a map is a direction.

A map imposes no will on anyone, breaks no one in to its "policy." And yet we obey our maps.

The will to have the map full, accurate, and up to date, and the determination to have its indications respected, would have to pervade the whole community. To nourish and sustain that will must be the task not of any particular social or economic division of the community, but of the whole body of right-minded people in that community. The organization and preservation of that power of will is the primary undertaking, therefore, of a world revolution aiming at universal peace, welfare and happy activity. And through that will it will produce as the central organ the brain of the modern community, a great encyclopaedic organization, kept constantly up to date and giving approximate estimates and directions for all the material activities of mankind.

The older and still prevalent conception of government is bullying, is the breaking-in and subjugation of the "subject," to the God, or king, or lords of the community. Will-bending, the overcoming of the recalcitrant junior and inferior, was an essential process in the establishment of primitive societies, and its tradition still rules our education and law. No doubt there must be a necessary accommodation of the normal human will to every form of society; no man is innately virtuous; but compulsion and restraint are the friction of the social machine and, other things being equal, the less compulsive social arrangements are, the more willingly, naturally, and easily they are accepted, the less wasteful of moral effort and the happier that community will be. The ideal state, other things being equal, is the state with the fewest possible number of will fights and will suppressions. This must be a primary consideration in arranging the economic, biological, and mental organization of the world community at which we aim.

We have advanced the opinion that the control of population pressure is practicable without any violent conflict with "human nature," that given a proper atmosphere of knowledge and intention, there need be far less suppression of will in relation to production than prevails to-day. In the same way, it is possible that the general economic life of mankind may be made universally satisfactory, that there may be an abundance out of all comparison greater than the existing supply of things necessary for human well-being, freedom, and activity, with not merely not more, but infinitely less subjugation and enslavement than now occurs. Man is still but half born out of the blind struggle for existence, and his nature still partakes of the infinite wastefulness of his mother Nature. He has still to learn how to price the commodities he covets in terms of human life. He is indeed only beginning to realize that there is anything to be learnt in that matter. He wastes will and human possibility extravagantly in his current economic methods.

We know nowadays that the nineteenth century expended a great wealth of intelligence upon a barren controversy between Individualism and Socialism. They were treated as mutually exclusive alternatives, instead of being questions of degree. Human society has been, is, and always must be an intricate system of adjustments between unconditional liberty and the disciplines and subordinations of co-operative enterprise. Affairs do not move simply from a more individualist to a more socialist state or vice versa; there may be a release of individual initiative going on here and standardization or restraint increasing there. Personal property never can be socially guaranteed and yet remain unlimited in action and extent as the extremer individualists desired, nor can it be "abolished" as the extremer socialists proposed. Property is not robbery, as Proudhon asserted; it is the protection of things against promiscuous and mainly wasteful use. Property is not necessarily personal. In some cases property may restrict or forbid a use of things that would be generally advantageous, and it may be and is frequently unfair in its assignment of initiative, but the remedy for that is not an abolition but a revision of property. In the concrete it is a form necessary for liberty of action upon material, while abstracted as money, which is a liquidated generalized form of property; it is a ticket for individual liberty of movement and individual choice of reward.

The economic history of mankind is a history of the operation of the idea of property; it relates the conflict of the unlimited acquisitiveness of egoistic individuals against the resentment of the disinherited and unsuccessful and the far less effective consciousness of a general welfare. Money grew out of a system of abstracting conventions and has been subjected to a great variety of restrictions, monopolizations, and regulations. It has never been an altogether logical device, and it has permitted the most extensive and complex developments of credit, debt, and dispossession. All these developments have brought with them characteristic forms of misuse and corruption. The story is intricate, and the tangle of relationships, of dependence, of pressure, of interception, of misdirected services, crippling embarrassments, and crushing obligations in which we live to-day admits of no such simple and general solutions as many exponents of socialism, for example, seem to consider possible.

But the thought and investigations of the past century or so have made it clear that a classification of property, according to the nature of the rights exercisable and according to the range of ownership involved, must be the basis of any system of social justice in the future.

Certain things, the ocean, the air, rare wild animals, must be the collective property of all mankind and cannot be altogether safe until they are so regarded, and until some concrete body exists to exercise these proprietary rights. Whatever collective control exists must protect these universal properties, the sea from derelicts, the strange shy things of the wild from extermination by the hunter and the foolish collector. The extinction of many beautiful creatures is one of the penalties our world is paying for its sluggishness in developing a collective common rule. And there are many staple things and general needs that now also demand a unified control in the common interest. The raw material of the earth should be for all, not to be monopolized by any acquisitive individual or acquisitive sovereign state, and not to be withheld from exploitation for the general benefit of any chance claims to territorial priority of this or that backward or bargaining person or tribe.

In the past, most of these universal concerns have had to be left to the competitive enterprise of profit-seeking individuals because there were as yet no collectivities organized to the pitch of ability needed to develop and control these concerns, but surely nobody in his senses believes that the supply and distribution of staple commodities about the earth by irresponsible persons and companies working entirely for monetary gain is the best possible method from the point of view of the race as a whole. The land of the earth, all utilizable natural products, have fallen very largely under the rules and usages of personal property because in the past that was the only recognized and practicable form of administrative proprietorship. The development both of extensive proprietary companies and of government departments with economic functions has been a matter of the last few centuries, the development, that is to say, of communal, more or less impersonal ownership, and it is only through these developments that the idea of organized collectivity of proprietorship has become credible.

Even in quite modern state enterprises there is a tendency to recall the role of the vigilant, jealous, and primitive personal proprietor in the fiction of ownership by His Majesty the King. In Great Britain, for example, Georgius Rex is still dimly supposed to hover over the Postmaster General of his Post Office, approve, disapprove, and call him to account. But the Postal Union of the world which steers a registered letter from Chile to Norway or from Ireland to Pekin is almost completely divorced from the convention of an individual owner. It works; it is criticized without awe or malice. Except for the stealing and steaming of letters practised by the political police of various countries, it works fairly well. And the only force behind it to keep it working well is the conscious common sense of mankind.

But when we have stipulated for the replacement of individual private ownership by more highly organized forms of collective ownership, subject to free criticism and responsible to the whole republic of mankind, in the general control of sea and land, in the getting, preparation, and distribution of staple products and in transport, we have really named all the possible generalizations of concrete ownership that the most socialistic of contemporaries will be disposed to demand. And if we add to that the necessary maintenance of a money system by a central world authority upon a basis that will make money keep faith with the worker who earns it, and represent from first to last for him the value in staple commodities he was given to understand it was to have, and if we conceive credit adequately controlled in the general interest by a socialized world banking organization, we shall have defined the entire realm from which individual property and unrestricted individual enterprise have been excluded. Beyond that, the science of social psychology will probably assure us that the best work will be done for the world by individuals free to exploit their abilities as they wish. If the individual landowner or mineral-owner disappears altogether from the world, he will probably be replaced over large areas by tenants with considerable security of tenure, by householders and by licensees under collective proprietors. It will be the practice, the recognized best course, to allow the cultivator to profit as fully as possible by his own individual productivity and to leave the householder to fashion his house and garden after his own desire.

Such in the very broadest terms is the character of the world commonweal towards which the modern imagination is moving, so far as its direction and economic life are concerned. The organization of collective bodies capable of exercising these wider proprietorships, which cannot be properly used in the common interest by uncorrelated individual owners, is the positive practical problem before the intelligent portion of mankind to-day. The nature of such collective bodies is still a series of open questions, even upon such points as whether they will be elected bodies or groups deriving their authority from other sanctions. Their scope and methods of operation, their relations to one another and to the central bureau of intelligence remain also to be defined. But before we conclude this essay we may be able to find precisions for at least the beginning of such definition.

Nineteenth-century socialism in its various forms, including the highly indurated formulae of communism, has been a series of projects for the establishment of such collective controls, for the most part very sketchy projects from which the necessary factor of a sound psychological analysis was almost completely wanting. Primarily movements of protest and revolt against the blazing injustices arising out of the selfishly individualistic exploitation of the new and more productive technical and financial methods of the eighteenth and nineteenth centuries, they have been apt to go beyond the limits of reasonable socialization in their demands and to minimize absurdly the difficulties and dangers of collective control. Indignation and impatience were their ruling moods, and if they constructed little they exposed much. We are better able to measure the magnitude of the task before us because of the clearances and lessons achieved by these pioneer movements.

IX

No Stable Utopia Is Now Conceivable

This unified world towards which the Open Conspiracy would direct its activities cannot be pictured for the reader as any static and stereotyped spectacle of happiness. Indeed, one may doubt if such a thing as happiness is possible without steadily changing conditions involving continually enlarging and exhilarating opportunities. Mankind, released from the pressure of population, the waste of warfare and the private monopolization of the sources of wealth, will face the universe with a great and increasing surplus of will and energy. Change and novelty will be the order of life; each day will differ from its predecessor in its great amplitude of interest. Life which was once routine, endurance, and mischance will become adventure and discovery. It will no longer be "the old, old story."

We have still barely emerged from among the animals in their struggle for existence. We live only in the early dawn of human self-consciousness and in the first awakening of the spirit of mastery. We believe that the persistent exploration of our outward and inward worlds by scientific and artistic endeavour will lead to developments of power and activity upon which at present we can set no limits nor give any certain form.

Our antagonists are confusion of mind, want of courage, want of curiosity and want of imagination, indolence, and spendthrift egotism. These are the enemies against which the Open Conspiracy arrays itself; these are the jailers of human freedom and achievement.

X

THE OPEN CONSPIRACY IS NOT TO BE THOUGHT OF AS A SINGLE ORGANIZATION; IT IS A CONCEPTION OF LIFE OUT OF WHICH EFFORTS, ORGANIZATIONS, AND NEW ORIENTATIONS WILL ARISE

This open and declared intention of establishing a world order out of the present patchwork of particularist governments, of effacing the militarist conceptions that have hitherto given governments their typical form, and of removing credit and the broad fundamental processes of economic life out of reach of private profit-seeking and individual monopolization, which is the substance of this Open Conspiracy to which the modern religious mind must necessarily address its practical activities, cannot fail to arouse enormous opposition. It is not a creative effort in a clear field; it is a creative effort that can hardly stir without attacking established things. It is the repudiation of drift, of "leaving things alone." It criticizes everything in human life from the top to the bottom and finds everything not good enough. It strikes at the universal human desire to feel that things are "all right."

One might conclude, and it would be a hasty, unsound conclusion, that the only people to whom we could look for sympathy and any passionate energy in forwarding the revolutionary change would be the unhappy, the discontented, the dispossessed, and the defeated in life's struggle. This idea lies at the root of the class-war dogmas of the Marxists, and it rests on an entirely crude conception of human nature. The successful minority is supposed to have no effective motive but a desire to retain and intensify its advantages. A quite imaginary solidarity to that end is attributed to it, a preposterous, base class activity. On the other hand, the unsuccessful mass – "proletariat" – is supposed to be capable of a clear apprehension of its disadvantages, and the more it is impoverished and embittered, the clearer-minded it becomes, and the nearer draws its uprising, its constructive "dictatorship," and the Millenium.

No doubt a considerable amount of truth is to be found in this theory of the Marxist revolution. Human beings, like other animals, are disposed to remain where their circumstances are tolerable and to want change when they are uncomfortable, and so a great proportion of the people who are "well off" want little or no change in present conditions, particularly those who are too dull to be bored by an unprogressive life, while a great proportion of those who actually feel the inconveniences of straitened means and population pressure, do. But much vaster masses of the rank and file of humanity are accustomed to inferiority and dispossession, they do not feel these things to the extent even of desiring change, or even if they do feel their disadvantages, they still fear change more than they dislike their disadvantages. Moreover, those who are sufficiently distressed to realize that "something ought to be done about it" are much more disposed to childish and threatening demands upon heaven and the government for redress and vindictive and punitive action against the envied fortunate with whom they happen to be in immediate contact, than to any reaction towards such complex, tentative, disciplined constructive work as alone can better the lot of mankind. In practice Marxism is found to work out in a ready resort to malignantly destructive activities, and to be so uncreative as to be practically impotent in the face of material difficulties. In Russia, where – in and about the urban centres, at least – Marxism has been put to the test, the doctrine of the Workers' Republic remains as a unifying cant, a test of orthodoxy of as little practical significance there as the communism of Jesus and communion with Christ in Christendom, while beneath this creed a small oligarchy which has attained power by its profession does its obstinate best, much hampered by the suspicion and hostility of the Western financiers and politicians, to carry on a series of interesting and varyingly successful experiments in the socialization of economic life. Here we have no scope to discuss the N. E. P. and the Five Year Plan. They are dealt with in *The Work, Wealth, and Happiness of Mankind*. Neither was properly Communist. The Five Year Plan is carried out as an autocratic state capitalism. Each year shows more and more clearly that Marxism and Communism are divagations from the path of human progress and that the line of advance must follow a course more intricate and less flattering to the common impulses of our nature.

The one main strand of truth in the theory of social development woven by Marx and Engels is that successful, comfortable people are disposed to dislike, obstruct and even resist actively any substantial changes in the current patchwork of arrangements, however great the ultimate dangers of that patchwork may be or the privations and sufferings of other people involved in it. The one main strand of error in that theory is the facile assumption that the people at a disadvantage will be stirred to anything more than chaotic and destructive expressions of resentment. If now we reject the error and accept the truth, we lose the delusive comfort of belief in that magic giant, the Proletariat, who will dictate, arrange, restore, and create, but we clear the way for the recognition of an elite of intelligent, creative-minded people scattered through the whole community, and for a study of the method of making this creative element effective in human affairs against the massive oppositions of selfishness and unimaginative self-protective conservatism.

Now, certain classes of people such as thugs and burglars seem to be harmful to society without a redeeming point about them, and others, such as racecourse bookmakers, seem to provide the minimum of distraction and entertainment with a maximum of mischief. Wilful idlers are a mere burthen on the community. Other social classes again, professional soldiers, for example, have a certain traditional honourableness which disguises the essentially parasitic relationship of their services to the developing modern community. Armies and armaments are cancers produced by the malignant development of the patriotic virus under modern conditions of exaggeration and mass suggestion. But since there are armies prepared to act coercively in the world to-day, it is necessary that the Open Conspiracy should develop within itself the competence to resist military coercion and combat and destroy armies that stand in the way of its emergence. Possibly the first two types here instanced may be condemned as classes and excluded as classes from any participation in the organized effort to recast the world but quite obviously the soldier cannot. The world commonweal will need its own scientific methods of protection so long as there are people running about the planet with flags and uniforms and weapons, offering violence to their fellow men and interfering with the free movements of commodities in the name of national sovereignty.

And when we come to the general functioning classes, landowners, industrial organizers, bankers, and so forth, who control the present system, such as it is, it should be still plainer that it is very largely from the ranks of these classes, and from their stores of experience and traditions of method, that the directive forces of the new order must emerge. The Open Conspiracy can have nothing to do with the heresy that the path of human progress lies through an extensive class war.

Let us consider, for example, how the Open Conspiracy stands to such a complex of activities, usages, accumulations, advantages as constitutes the banking world. There are no doubt many bankers and many practices in banking which make for personal or group advantage to the general detriment. They forestall, monopolize, constrain, and extort, and so increase their riches. And another large part of that banking world follows routine and established usage; it is carrying on and keeping things going, and it is neither inimical nor conducive to the development of a progressive world organization of finance. But there remains a residuum of original and intelligent people in banking or associated with banking or mentally interested in banking, who do realize that banking plays a very important and interesting part in the world's affairs, who are curious about their own intricate function and disposed towards a scientific investigation of its origins, conditions, and future possibilities. Such types move naturally towards the Open Conspiracy. Their enquiries carry them inevitably outside the bankers' habitual field to an examination of the nature, drift, and destiny of the entire economic process.

Now the theme of the preceding paragraph might be repeated with variations through a score of paragraphs in which appropriate modifications would adapt it to the industrial organizer, the merchant and organizer of transport, the advertiser, the retail distributor, the agriculturalist, the engineer, the builder, the economic chemist, and a number of other types functional in the contemporary community. In all we should distinguish firstly, a base and harmful section, then a mediocre section following established usage, and lastly, an active, progressive section to whom we turn naturally for developments leading towards the progressive world commonweal of our desires. And our analysis might penetrate further than separation into types of individuals. In nearly every individual instance we should find a mixed composition, a human being of fluctuating moods and confused purposes, sometimes base, sometimes drifting with the tide and sometimes alert and intellectually and morally quickened. The Open Conspiracy must be content to take a fraction of a man, as it appeals to fractions of many classes, if it cannot get him altogether.

This idea of drawing together a proportion of all or nearly all the functional classes in contemporary communities in order to weave the beginnings of a world community out of their selection is a fairly obvious one – and yet it has still to win practical recognition. Man is a morbidly gregarious and partisan creature; he is deep in his immediate struggles and stands by his own kind because in so doing he defends himself; the industrialist is best equipped to criticize his fellow industrialist, but he finds the root of all evil in the banker; the wages worker shifts the blame for all social wrongs on the "employing class." There is an element of exasperation in most economic and social reactions, and there is hardly a reforming or revolutionary movement in history which is not essentially an indiscriminate attack of one functioning class or type upon another, on the assumption that the attacked class is entirely to blame for the clash and that the attacking class is self-sufficient in the commonweal and can dispense with its annoying collaborator. A considerable element of justice usually enters into such recriminations. But the Open Conspiracy cannot avail itself of these class animosities for its driving force. It can have, therefore, no uniform method of approach. For each class it has a conception of modification and development, and each class it approaches therefore at a distinctive angle. Some classes, no doubt, it would supersede altogether; others – the scientific investigator, for example – it must regard as almost wholly good and seek only to multiply and empower, but it can no more adopt the prejudices and extravagances of any particular class as its basis than it can adopt the claims of any existing state or empire.

When it is clearly understood that the binding links of the Open Conspiracy we have in mind are certain broad general ideas, and that – except perhaps in the case of scientific workers – we have no current set of attitudes of mind and habits of activity which we can turn over directly and unmodified to the service of the conspiracy, we are in a position to realize that the movement we contemplate must from the outset be diversified in its traditions and elements and various in its methods. It must fight upon several fronts and with many sorts of equipment. It will have a common spirit, but it is quite conceivable that between many of its contributory factors there may be very wide gaps in understanding and sympathy. It is no sort of simple organization.

XI

FORCES AND RESISTANCES IN THE GREAT MODERN COMMUNITIES NOW PREVALENT, WHICH ARE ANTAGONISTIC TO THE OPEN CONSPIRACY. THE WAR WITH TRADITION

We have now stated broadly but plainly the idea of the world commonweal which is the objective of the Open Conspiracy, and we have made a preliminary examination of the composition of that movement, showing that it must be necessarily not a class development, but a convergence of many different sorts of people upon a common idea. Its opening task must be the elaboration, exposition, and propaganda of this common idea, a steady campaign to revolutionize education and establish a modern ideology in men's minds and, arising out of this, the incomparably vaster task of the realization of its ideas.

These are tasks not to be done *in vacuo*; they have to be done in a dense world of crowding, incessant, passionate, unco-ordinated activities, the world of market and newspaper, seed-time and harvest, births, deaths, jails, hospitals, riots, barracks and army manoeuvres, false prophets and royal processions, games and shows, fire, storm, pestilence, earthquake, war. Every day and every hour things will be happening to help or thwart, stimulate or undermine, obstruct or defeat the creative effort to set up the world commonweal.

Before we go on to discuss the selection and organization of these heterogeneous and mainly religious impulses upon which we rest our hopes of a greater life for mankind, before we plan how these impulses may be got together into a system of co-ordinated activities, it will be well to review the main antagonistic forces with which, from its very inception, the Open Conspiracy will be – is now – in conflict.

To begin with, we will consider these forces as they present themselves in the highly developed Western European States of to-day and in their American derivatives, derivatives which, in spite of the fact that in most cases they have far outgrown their lands of origin, still owe a large part of their social habits and political conceptions to Europe. All these States touch upon the Atlantic or its contributory seas; they have all grown to their present form since the discovery of America; they have a common tradition rooting in the ideas of

Christendom and a generic resemblance of method. Economically and socially they present what is known in current parlance as the Capitalist system, but it will relieve us of a considerable load of disputatious matter if we call them here simply the "Atlantic" civilizations and communities.

The consideration of these Atlantic civilizations in relation to the coming world civilization will suffice for the present chapter. Afterwards we will consider the modification of the forces antagonistic to the Open Conspiracy as they display themselves beyond the formal confines of these now dominant states in the world's affairs, in the social systems weakened and injured by their expansion, and among such less highly organized communities as still survive from man's savage and barbaric past.

The Open Conspiracy is not necessarily antagonistic to any existing government. The Open Conspiracy is a creative, organizing movement and not an anarchistic one. It does not want to destroy existing controls and forms of human association, but either to supersede or amalgamate them into a common world directorate. If constitutions, parliaments, and kings can be dealt with as provisional institutions, trustees for the coming of age of the world commonweal, and in so far as they are conducted in that spirit, the Open Conspiracy makes no attack upon them.

But most governments will not set about their business as in any way provisional; they and their supporters insist upon a reverence and obedience which repudiate any possibility of supersession. What should be an instrument becomes a divinity. In nearly every country of the world there is, in deference to the pretended necessities of a possible war, a vast degrading and dangerous cultivation of loyalty and mechanical subservience to flags, uniforms, presidents, and kings. A president or king who does his appointed work well and righteously is entitled to as much subservience as a bricklayer who does his work well and righteously and to no more, but instead there is a sustained endeavour to give him the privileges of an idol above criticism or reproach, and the organized worship of flags has become – with changed conditions of intercourse and warfare – an entirely evil misdirection of the gregarious impulses of our race. Emotion and sentimentality are evoked in the cause of disciplines and co-operations that could quite easily be sustained and that are better sustained by rational conviction.

The Open Conspiracy is necessarily opposed to all such implacable loyalties, and still more so to the aggressive assertion and propaganda of such loyalties. When these things take the form of suppressing reasonable criticism and forbidding even the suggestion of other forms of government, they become plainly antagonists to any comprehensive project for human welfare. They become manifestly, from the wider point of view, seditious, and loyalty to "king and country" passes into plain treason to mankind. Almost everywhere, at present, educational institutions organize barriers in the path of progress, and there are only the feeblest attempts at any counter education that will break up these barriers. There is little or no effort to restrain the aggressive nationalist when he waves his flag against the welfare of our race, or to protect the children of the world from the infection of his enthusiasms. And this last is as true now of the American system as it is of any European State.

In the great mass of the modern community there is little more than a favourable acquiescence in patriotic ideas and in the worship of patriotic symbols, and that is based largely on such training. These things are not necessary things for the generality of to-day. A change of mental direction would be possible for the majority of people now without any violent disorganization of their intimate lives or any serious social or economic readjustments for them. Mental infection in such cases could be countered by mental sanitation. A majority of people in Europe, and a still larger majority in the United States and the other American Republics, could become citizens of the world without any serious hindrance to their present occupations, and with an incalculably vast increase of their present security.

But there remains a net of special classes in every community, from kings to custom-house officers, far more deeply involved in patriotism because it is their trade and their source of honour, and prepared in consequence with an instinctive resistance to any reorientation of ideas towards a broader outlook. In the case of such people no mental sanitation is possible without dangerous and alarming changes in their way of living. For the majority of these patriots by *métier*, the Open Conspiracy unlocks the gates leading from a fussy paradise of eminence, respect, and privilege, and motions them towards an austere wilderness which does not present even the faintest promise of a congenial, distinguished life for them. Nearly everything in human nature will dispose them to turn away from these gates which open towards the world peace, to bang-to and lock them again if they can, and to grow thickets as speedily as possible to conceal them and get them forgotten. The suggestion of being trustees in a transition will seem to most of such people only the camouflage of an ultimate degradation.

From such classes of patriots by *métier*, it is manifest that the Open Conspiracy can expect only opposition. It may detach individuals from them, but only by depriving them of their essential class loyalties and characteristics. The class as a class will remain none the less antagonistic. About royal courts and presidential residences, in diplomatic, consular, military, and naval circles, and wherever people wear titles and uniforms and enjoy pride and precedences based on existing political institutions, there will be the completest general inability to grasp the need for the Open Conspiracy. These people and their womankind, their friends and connections, their servants and dependents, are fortified by time-honoured traditions of social usage, of sentiment and romantic prestige. They will insist that they are reality and Cosmopolis a dream. Only individuals of exceptional liveliness, rare intellectual power, and innate moral force can be expected to break away from the anti-progressive habits such class conditions impose upon them.

This tangle of traditions and loyalties, of interested trades and professions, of privileged classes and official patriots, this complex of human beings embodying very easy and natural and time-honoured ideas of eternal national separation and unending international and class conflict, is the main objective of the Open Conspiracy in its opening phase. This tangle must be disentangled as the Open Conspiracy advances, and until it is largely disentangled and cleared up that Open Conspiracy cannot become anything very much more than a desire and a project.

This tangle of "necessary patriots," as one may call them, is different in its nature, less intricate and extensive proportionally in the United States and the States of Latin America, than it is in the old European communities, but it is none the less virulent in its action on that account. It is only recently that military and naval services have become important factors in American social life, and the really vitalizing contact of the interested patriot and the State has hitherto centred mainly upon the custom house and the concession. Instead of a mellow and romantic loyalty to "king and country" the American thinks simply of America and his flag.

The American exaggeration of patriotism began as a resistance to exploitation from overseas. Even when political and fiscal freedom were won, there was a long phase of industrial and financial dependence. The American's habits of mind, in spite of his recent realization of the enormous power and relative prosperity of the United States and of the expanding possibilities of their Spanish and Portuguese-speaking neighbours, are still largely self-protective against a now imaginary European peril. For the first three quarters of the nineteenth century the people of the American continent, and particularly the people of the United States, felt the industrial and financial ascendancy of Great Britain and had a reasonable fear of European attacks upon their continent. A growing tide of immigrants of uncertain sympathy threatened their dearest habits. Flag worship was imposed primarily as a repudiation of Europe. Europe no longer looms over America with overpowering intimations, American industries no longer have any practical justification for protection, American finance would be happier without it, but the patriotic interests are so established now that they go on and will go on. No American statesman who ventures to be cosmopolitan in his utterance and outlook is likely to escape altogether from the raucous attentions of the patriotic journalist.

We have said that the complex of classes in any country interested in the current method of government is sustained by traditions and impelled by its nature and conditions to protect itself against exploratory criticism. It is therefore unable to escape from the forms of competitive and militant nationalism in which it was evolved. It cannot, without grave danger of enfeeblement, change any such innate form. So that while parallel complexes of patriotic classes are found in greater or less intricacy grouped about the flags and governments of most existing states, these complexes are by their nature obliged to remain separate, nationalist, and mutually antagonistic. You cannot expect a world union of soldiers or diplomatists. Their existence and nature depend upon the idea that national separation is real and incurable, and that war, in the long run, is unavoidable. Their conceptions of loyalty involve an antagonism to all foreigners, even to foreigners of exactly the same types as themselves, and make for a continual campaign of annoyances, suspicions, and precautions – together with a general propaganda, affecting all other classes, of the necessity of an international antagonism – that creeps persistently towards war.

But while the methods of provoking war employed by the patriotic classes are traditional, modern science has made a new and enormously more powerful thing of warfare and, as the Great War showed, even the most conservative generals on both sides are unable to prevent the gigantic interventions of the mechanician and the chemist. So that a situation is brought about in which the militarist element is unable to fight without the support of the modern industrial organization and the acquiescence of the great mass of people. We are confronted therefore at the present time with the paradoxical situation that a patriotic tradition sustains in power and authority warlike classes who are quite incapable of carrying on war. The other classes to which they must go for support when the disaster of war is actually achieved are classes developed under peace conditions, which not only have no positive advantage in war, but must, as a whole, suffer great dislocation, discomfort, destruction, and distress from war. It is of primary importance therefore, to the formally dominant classes that these new social masses and powers should remain under the sway of the old social, sentimental, and romantic traditions, and equally important is it to the Open Conspiracy that they should be released.

Here we bring into consideration another great complex of persons, interests, traditions – the world of education, the various religious organizations, and, beyond these, the ramifying, indeterminate world of newspapers and other periodicals, books, the drama, art, and all the instruments of presentation and suggestion that mould opinion and direct action. The sum of the operations of this complex will be either to sustain or to demolish the old nationalist militant ascendancy. Its easiest immediate course is to accept it. Educational organizations on that account are now largely a conservative force in the community; they are in most cases directly controlled by authority and bound officially as well as practically to respect current fears and prejudices. It evokes fewer difficulties for them if they limit and mould rather than release the young. The schoolmaster tends, therefore, to accept and standardize and stereotype, even in the living, progressive fields of science and philosophy. Even there he is a brake on the forward movement. It is clear that the Open Conspiracy must either continually disturb and revivify him or else frankly antagonize him. Universities also struggle between the honourable past on which their prestige rests, and the need of adaptation to a world of enquiry, experiment, and change. It is an open question whether these particular organizations of intellectual prestige are of any real value in the living world. A modern world planned *de novo* would probably produce nothing like a contemporary university. Modern research, one may argue, would be stimulated rather than injured by complete detachment from the lingering mediaevalism of such institutions, their entanglement with adolescent education, and their ancient and contagious conceptions of precedence and honour.

Ordinary religious organizations, again, exist for self-preservation and are prone to follow rather than direct the currents of popular thought. They are kept alive, indeed, by revivalism and new departures which at the outset they are apt to resist, as the Catholic Church, for instance, resisted the Franciscan awakening, but their formal disposition is conservative. They say to religious development, thus far and no farther.

Here, in school, college, and church, are activities of thought and instruction which, generally speaking, drag upon the wheels of progress, but which need not necessarily do so. A schoolmaster may be original, stimulating, and creative, and if he is fortunate and a good fighter he may even achieve considerable worldly success; university teachers and investigators may strike out upon new lines and yet escape destruction by the older dons. Universities compete against other universities at home and abroad and cannot altogether yield to the forces of dullness and subservience. They must maintain a certain difference from vulgar opinion and a certain repute of intellectual virility.

As we pass from the more organized to the less organized intellectual activities, we find conservative influence declining in importance, and a freer play for the creative drive. Freshness is a primary condition of journalistic, literary, and artistic success, and orthodoxy has nothing new to say or do. But the desire for freshness may be satisfied all too readily by merely extravagant, superficial, and incoherent inventions.

The influence of this old traditional nationalist social and political hierarchy which blocks the way to the new world is not, however, exerted exclusively through its control over schools and universities. Nor is that indeed its more powerful activity. Would that it were! There is also a direct, less defined contact of the old order with the nascent powers, that plays a far more effective part in delaying the development of the modern world commonweal. Necessarily the old order has determined the established way of life, which is, at its best, large, comfortable, amusing, respected. It possesses all the entrances and exits and all the controls of the established daily round. It is able to exact, and it does exact, almost without design, many conformities. There can be no very ample social life, therefore, for those who are conspicuously dissentient. Again the old order has a complete provision for the growth, welfare, and advancement of its children. It controls the founts of honour and self-respect; it provides a mapped-out world of behaviour. The new initiatives make their appearance here and there in the form of isolated individuals, here an inventor, there a bold organizer or a vigorous thinker. Apart from his specific work the innovating type finds that he must fall in with established things or his womenfolk will be ostracized, and he will be distressed by a sense of isolation even in the midst of successful activities. The more intensely he innovates in partic-ular, the more likely is he to be too busy to seek out kindred souls and organize a new social life in general. The new things and ideas, even when they arise abundantly, arise scattered and unorganized, and the old order takes them in its net. America for example – both on its Latin and on its English-speaking side – is in many ways a triumph of the old order over the new.

Men like Winwood Reade thought that the New World would be indeed a new world. They idealized its apparent emancipations. But as the more suc-cessful of the toiling farmers and traders of republican America rose one by one to affluence, leisure, and freedom, it was far more easy for them to adopt the polished and prepared social patterns and usages of Europe than to work out a new civilization in accordance with their equalitarian professions. Yet there remains a gap in their adapted "Society." Henry James, that acute observer of subtle social flavours, has pointed out the peculiar *headlessness* of social life in America because of the absence of court functions to "go on" to and justify the assembling and dressing. The social life has imitated the prepa-ration for the Court without any political justification. In Europe the assimila-tion of the wealthy European industrialist and financier by the old order has been parallel and naturally more logically complete. He really has found a court to "go on" to. His social scheme was still undecapitated until kingdoms began to change into republics after 1917.

In this way the complex of classes vitally involved in the old militant nationalist order is mightily reinforced by much larger masses of imitative and annexed and more or less assimilated rich and active people. The great indus-trialist has married the daughter of the marquis and has a couple of sons in the Guards and a daughter who is a princess. The money of the American Leeds, fleeing from the social futility of its land of origin, helped bolster up a mis-chievous monarchy in Greece. The functional and private lives of the new men are thus at war with one another. The real interests of the great industrialist or financier lie in cosmopolitan organization and the material development of the world commonweal, but his womenfolk pin flags all over him, and his sons are prepared to sacrifice themselves and all his business creations for the sake of trite splendours and Ruritanian romance.

But just so far as the great business organizer is capable and creative, so far is he likely to realize and resent the price in frustration that the old order obliges him to pay for amusement, social interest, and domestic peace and comfort. The Open Conspiracy threatens him with no effacement; it may even appear with an air of release. If he had women who were interested in his business affairs instead of women who had to be amused, and if he realized in time the practical, intellectual, and moral kidnapping of his sons and daugh-ters by the old order that goes on, he might pass quite easily from acquiescence to antagonism. But in this respect he cannot act single-handed. This is a social and not an individual operation. The Open Conspiracy, it is clear, must include in its activities a great fight for the souls of economically-functional people. It must carve out a Society of its own from Society. Only by the creation of a new and better social life can it resist the many advantages and attractions of the old.

This constant gravitation back to traditional uses on the part of what might become new social types applies not merely to big people but to such small people as are really functional in the modern economic scheme. They have no social life adapted to their new economic relationships, and they are forced back upon the methods of behaviour established for what were roughly their analogues in the old order of things. The various sorts of managers and foremen in big modern concerns, for example, carry on ways of living they have taken ready-made from the stewards, tradesmen, tenantry, and upper servants of an aristocratic territorial system, They release themselves and are released almost in spite of themselves, slowly, generation by generation, from habits of social subservience that are no longer necessary nor convenient in the social process, acquire an official pride in themselves and take on new conceptions of responsible loyalty to a scheme. And they find themselves under suggestions of class aloofness and superiority to the general mass of less cardinal workers, that are often unjustifiable under new conditions. Machinery and scientific organization have been and still are revolutionizing productive activity by the progressive elimination of the unskilled worker, the hack, the mere toiler. But the social organization of the modern community and the mutual deportment of the associated workers left over after this elimination are still haunted by the tradition of the lord, the middle-class tenant, and the servile hind. The development of self-respect and mutual respect among the mass of modern functional workers is clearly an intimate concern of the Open Conspiracy.

A vast amount of moral force has been wasted in the past hundred years by the antagonism of "Labour" to "Capital," as though this were the primary issue in human affairs. But this never was the primary issue, and it is steadily receding from its former importance. The ancient civilizations did actually rest upon a broad basis of slavery and serfdom. Human muscle was a main source of energy – ranking with sun, wind, and flood. But invention and discovery have so changed the conditions under which power is directed and utilized that muscle becomes economically secondary and inessential. We no longer want hewers of wood and drawers of water, carriers and pick and spade men. We no longer want that breeding swarm of hefty sweaty bodies without which the former civilizations could not have endured. We want watchful and understanding guardians and drivers of complex delicate machines, which can be mishandled and brutalized and spoilt all too easily. The less disposed these masters of our machines are to inordinate multiplication, the more room and food in the world for their ampler lives. Even to the lowest level of a fully-mechanicalized civilization it is required that the human element should be select. In the modern world, crowds are a survival, and they will presently be an anachronism, and crowd psychology therefore cannot supply the basis of a new order.

It is just because labour is becoming more intelligent, responsible, and individually efficient that it is becoming more audible and impatient in social affairs. It is just because it is no longer mere gang labour, and is becoming more and more intelligent co-operation in detail, that it now resents being treated as a serf, housed like a serf, fed like a serf, and herded like a serf, and its pride and thoughts and feelings disregarded. Labour is in revolt because as a matter of fact it is, in the ancient and exact sense of the word, ceasing to be labour at all.

The more progressive elements of the directive classes recognize this, but, as we have shown, there are formidable forces still tending to maintain the old social attitudes when arrogance became the ruler and the common man accepted his servile status. A continual resistance is offered by large sections of the prosperous and advantaged to the larger claims of the modernized worker, and in response the rising and differentiating workers develop an angry antagonism to these directive classes which allow themselves to be controlled by their conservative and reactionary elements. Moreover, the increasing relative intelligence of the labour masses, the unprecedented imaginative stimulation they experience, the continually more widespread realization of the available freedoms and comforts and indulgences that might be and are not shared by all in a modern state, develop a recalcitrance where once there was little but fatalistic acquiescence. An objection to direction and obligation, always mutely present in the toiling multitude since the economic life of man began, becomes articulate and active. It is the taste of freedom that makes labour desire to be free. This series of frictions is a quite inevitable aspect of social reorganization, but it does not constitute a primary antagonism in the process.

The class war was invented by the classes; it is a natural tradition of the upper strata of the old order. It was so universally understood that there was no need to state it. It is implicit in nearly all the literature of the world before the nineteenth century – except the Bible, the Koran, and other sequelae. The "class war" of the Marxist is merely a poor snobbish imitation, a *tu quoque*, a pathetic, stupid, indignant reversal of and retort to the old arrogance, a pathetic *upward* arrogance.

These conflicts cut across rather than oppose or help the progressive development to which the Open Conspiracy devotes itself. Labour, awakened, enquiring, and indignant, is not necessarily progressive; if the ordinary undistingiushed worker is no longer to be driven as a beast of burthen, he has – which also goes against the grain – to be educated to as high a level of co-operative efficiency as possible. He has to work better, even if he works for much shorter hours and under better conditions, and his work must be subordinated work still; he cannot become *en masse* sole owner and master of a scheme of things he did not make and is incapable of directing. Yet this is the ambition implicit in an exclusively "Labour" movement. Either the Labour revolutionary hopes to cadge the services of exceptional people without acknowledgment or return on sentimental grounds, or he really believes that anyone is as capable as anyone else – if not more so. The worker at a low level may be flattered by dreams of "class-conscious" mass dominion from which all sense of inferiority is banished, but they will remain dreams. The deep instinctive jealousy of the commonplace individual for outstanding quality and novel initiative may be organized and turned to sabotage and destruction, masquerading as and aspiring to be a new social order, but that will be a blind alley and not the road of progress. Our hope for the human future does not lie in crowd psychology and the indiscriminating rule of universal democracy.

The Open Conspiracy can have little use for mere resentments as a driving force towards its ends; it starts with a proposal not to exalt the labour class but to abolish it, its sustaining purpose is to throw drudges out of employment and eliminate the inept – and it is far more likely to incur suspicion and distrust in the lower ranks of the developing industrial order of to-day than to win support there. There, just as everywhere else in the changing social complexes of our time, it can appeal only to the exceptionally understanding individual who can without personal humiliation consider his present activities and relationships as provisional and who can, without taking offence, endure a searching criticism of his present quality and mode of living.

XII

The Resistances Of The Less Industrialized Peoples To The Drive Of The Open Conspiracy

So far, in our accounting of the powers, institutions, dispositions, types, and classes which will be naturally opposed to the Open Conspiracy, we have surveyed only such territory in the domain of the future world commonweal as is represented by the complex, progressive, highly-industrialized communities, based on a preceding landlord-soldier, tenant, town-merchant, and trades-man system, of the Atlantic type. These communities have developed farthest in the direction of mechanicalization, and they are so much more efficient and powerful that they now dominate the rest of the world. India, China, Russia, Africa present *mélanges* of social systems, thrown together, outpaced, over-strained, shattered, invaded, exploited, and more or less subjugated by the finance, machinery, and political aggressions of the Atlantic, Baltic, and Mediterranean civilization. In many ways they have an air of assimilating themselves to that civilization, evolving modern types and classes, and abandoning much of their distinctive traditions. But what they take from the West is mainly the new developments, the material achievements, rather than the social and political achievements, that, empowered by modern inventions, have won their way to world predominance. They may imitate European nationalism to a certain extent; for them it becomes a convenient form of self-assertion against the pressure of a realized practical social and political inferiority; but the degree to which they will or can take over the social assumptions and habits of the long-established European-American hierarchy is probably very restricted. Their nationalism will remain largely indigenous; the social traditions to which they will try to make the new material forces subservient will be traditions of an Oriental life widely different from the original life of Europe. They will have their own resistances to the Open Conspiracy, there-fore, but they will be different resistances from those we have hitherto con-sidered. The automobile and the wireless set, the harvester and steel construction building, will come to the jungle rajah and the head hunter, the Brahmin and the Indian peasant, with a parallel and yet dissimilar message to the one they brought the British landowner or the corn and cattle farmers of the Argentine and the Middle West. Also they may be expected to evoke dissimilar reactions.

To a number of the finer, more energetic minds of these overshadowed communities which have lagged more or less in the material advances to which this present ascendancy of western Europe and America is due, the Open Conspiracy may come with an effect of immense invitation. At one step they may go from the sinking vessel of their antiquated order, across their present conquerors, into a brotherhood of world rulers. They may turn to the problem of saving and adapting all that is rich and distinctive of their inheritance to the common ends of the race. But to the less vigorous intelligences of this outer world, the new project of the Open Conspiracy will seem no better than a new form of Western envelopment, and they will fight a mighty liberation as though it were a further enslavement to the European tradition. They will watch the Open Conspiracy for any signs of conscious superiority and racial disregard. Necessarily they will recognize it as a product of Western mentality and they may well be tempted to regard it as an elaboration and organization of current dispositions rather than the evolution of a new phase which will make no discrimination at last between the effete traditions of either East or West. Their suspicions will be sustained and developed by the clumsy and muddle-headed political and economic aggressions of the contemporary political and business systems, such as they are, of the West, now in progress. Behind that cloud of aggression Western thought has necessarily advanced upon them. It could have got to their attention in no other way.

Partly these resistances and criticisms of the decadent communities outside the Atlantic capitalist systems will be aimed, not at the developing methods of the coming world community, but at the European traditions and restrictions that have imposed themselves upon these methods, and so far the clash of the East and West may be found to subserve the aims of the Open Conspiracy. In the conflict of old traditions and in the consequent deadlocks lies much hope for the direct acceptance of the groups of ideas centring upon the Open Conspiracy. One of the most interesting areas of humanity in this respect is the great system of communities under the sway or influence of Soviet Russia. Russia has never been completely incorporated with the European system; she became a just passable imitation of a western European monarchy in the seventeenth and eighteenth centuries, and talked at last of constitutions and parliaments – but the reality of that vast empire remained an Asiatic despotism, and the European mask was altogether smashed by the successive revolutions of 1917. The ensuing system is a government presiding over an enormous extent of peasants and herdsmen, by a disciplined association professing the faith and dogmas of Marx, as interpreted and qualified by Lenin and Stalin.

In many ways this government is a novelty of extraordinary interest. It labours against enormous difficulties within itself and without. Flung amazingly into a position of tremendous power, its intellectual flexibility is greatly restricted by the urgent militant necessity for mental unanimity and a consequent repression of criticism. It finds itself separated, intellectually and morally, by an enormous gap from the illiterate millions over which it rules. More open perhaps to scientific and creative conceptions than any other government, and certainly more willing to experiment and innovate, its enterprise is starved by the economic depletion of the country in the Great War and by the technical and industrial backwardness of the population upon which it must draw for its personnel. Moreover, it struggles within itself between concepts of a modern scientific social organization and a vague anarchistic dream in which the "State" is to disappear, and an emancipated proletariat, breeding and expectorating freely, fills the vistas of time forevermore. The tradition of long years of hopeless opposition has tainted the world policy of the Marxist cult with a mischievous and irritating quality that focuses upon it the animosity of every government in the dominant Atlantic system. Marxism never had any but the vaguest fancies about the relation of one nation to another, and the new Russian government, for all its cosmopolitan phrases, is more and more plainly the heir to the obsessions of Tsarist imperialism, using the Communist party, as other countries have used Christian missionaries, to maintain a propagandist government to forward its schemes. Nevertheless, the Soviet government has maintained itself for more than twelve years, and it seems far more likely to evolve than to perish. It is quite possible that it will evolve towards the conceptions of the Open Conspiracy, and in that case Russia may witness once again a conflict between new ideas and Old Believers. So far the Communist party in Moscow has maintained a considerable propaganda of ideas in the rest of the world and especially across its western frontier. Many of these ideas are now trite and stale. The time may be not far distant when the tide of propaganda will flow in the reverse direction. It has pleased the vanity of the Communist party to imagine itself conducting a propaganda of world revolution. Its fate may be to develop upon lines that will make its more intelligent elements easily assimilable to the Open Conspiracy for a world revolution. The Open Conspiracy as it spreads and grows may find a less encumbered field for trying out the economic developments implicit in its conceptions in Russia and Siberia than anywhere else in the world.

However severely the guiding themes and practical methods of the present Soviet government in Russia may be criticized, the fact remains that it has cleared out of its way many of the main obstructive elements that we find still vigorous in the more highly-organized communities in the West. It has liberated vast areas from the kindred superstitions of monarchy and the need for a private proprietary control of great economic interests. And it has presented both China and India with the exciting spectacle of a social and political system capable of throwing off many of the most characteristic features of triumphant Westernism, and yet holding its own. In the days when Japan faced up to modern necessities there were no models for imitation that were not communities of the Atlantic type pervaded by the methods of private capitalism, and in consequence the Japanese reconstituted their affairs on a distinctly European plan, adopting a Parliament and bringing their monarchy, social hierarchy, and business and financial methods into a general conformity with that model. It is extremely doubtful whether any other Asiatic community will now set itself to a parallel imitation, and it will be thanks largely to the Russian revolution that this breakaway from Europeanization has occurred.

But it does not follow that such a breakaway will necessarily lead more directly to the Open Conspiracy. If we have to face a less highly organized system of interests and prejudices in Russia and China, we have to deal with a vastly wider ignorance and a vastly more formidable animalism. Russia is a land of tens of millions of peasants ruled over by a little band of the intelligentsia who can be counted only by tens of thousands. It is only these few score thousands who are accessible to ideas of world construction, and the only hope of bringing the Russian system into active participation in the world conspiracy is through that small minority and through its educational repercussion on the myriads below. As we go eastward from European Russia the proportion of soundly prepared intelligence to which we can appeal for understanding and participation diminishes to an even more dismaying fraction. Eliminate that fraction, and one is left face to face with inchoate barbarism incapable of social and political organization above the level of the war boss and the brigand leader. Russia itself is still by no means secure against a degenerative process in that direction, and the hope of China struggling out of it without some forcible directive interventions is a hope to which constructive liberalism clings with very little assurance.

We turn back therefore from Russia, China and the communities of Central Asia to the Atlantic world. It is in that world alone that sufficient range and amplitude of thought and discussion are possible for the adequate development of the Open Conspiracy. In these communities it must begin and for a long time its main activities will need to be sustained from these necessary centres of diffusion. It will develop amidst incessant mental strife, and through that strife it will remain alive. It is no small part of the practical weakness of present-day communism that it attempts to centre its intellectual life and its directive activities in Moscow and so cuts itself off from the free and open discussions of the Western world. Marxism lost the world when it went to Moscow and took over the traditions of Tsarism, as Christianity lost the world when it went to Rome and took over the traditions of Caesar. Entrenched in Moscow from searching criticism, the Marxist ideology may become more and more dogmatic and unprogressive, repeating its sacred *credo* and issuing its disregarded orders to the proletariat of the world, and so stay ineffectively crystallized until the rising tide of the Open Conspiracy submerges, dissolves it afresh, and incorporates whatever it finds assimilable.

India, like Japan, is cut off from the main body of Asiatic affairs. But while Japan has become a formally Westernized nationality in the comity of such nations, India remains a world in itself. In that one peninsula nearly every type of community is to be found, from the tribe of jungle savages, through a great diversity of barbaric and mediaeval principalities, to the child and women-sweating factories and the vigorous modern commercialism of Bombay. Over it all the British imperialism prevails, a constraining and restraining influence, keeping the peace, checking epidemics, increasing the food supply by irrigation and the like, and making little or no effort to evoke responses to modern ideas. Britain in India is no propagandist of modern ferments: all those are left the other side of Suez. In India the Briton is a ruler as firm and self-assured and uncreative as the Roman. The old religious and social traditions, the complex customs, castes, tabus, and exclusions of a strangely-mixed but unamalgamated community, though a little discredited by this foreign predominance, still hold men's minds. They have been, so to speak, pickled in the preservative of the British raj.

The Open Conspiracy has to invade the Indian complex in conflict with the prejudices of both ruler and governed. It has to hope for individual breaches in the dull Romanism of the administration: here a genuine educationist, here a creative civil servant, here an official touched by the distant stir of the living homeland; and it has to try to bring these types into a co-operative relationship with a fine native scholar here or an active-minded prince or landowner or industrialist there. As the old methods of passenger transport are superseded by flying, it will be more and more difficult to keep the stir of the living homeland out of either the consciousness of the official hierarchy or the knowledge of the recalcitrant "native."

Very similar to Indian conditions is the state of affairs in the foreign possessions of France, the same administrative obstacles to the Open Conspiracy above, and below the same resentful subordination, cut off from the mental invigoration of responsibility. Within these areas of restraint, India and its lesser, simpler parallels in North Africa, Syria and the Far East, there goes on a rapid increase of low-grade population, undersized physically and mentally, and retarding the mechanical development of civilization by its standing offer of cheap labour to the unscrupulous entrepreneur, and possible feeble insurrectionary material to the unscrupulous political adventurer. It is impossible to estimate how slowly or how rapidly the knowledge and ideas that have checked the rate of increase of all the Atlantic populations may be diffused through these less alert communities.

We must complete our survey of the resistances against which the Open Conspiracy has to work by a few words about the Negro world and the regions of forest and jungle in which barbaric and even savage human life still escapes the infection of civilization. It seems inevitable that the development of modern means of communication and the conquest of tropical diseases should end in giving access everywhere to modern administration and to economic methods, and everywhere the incorporation of the former wilderness in the modern economic process means the destruction of the material basis, the free hunting, the free access to the soil, of such barbaric and savage communities as still precariously survive. The dusky peoples, who were formerly the lords of these still imperfectly assimilated areas, are becoming exploited workers, slaves, serfs, hut-tax payers, or labourers to a caste of white immigrants. The spirit of the plantation broods over all these lands. The Negro in America differs only from his subjugated brother in South Africa or Kenya Colony in the fact that he also, like his white master, is an immigrant. The situation in Africa and America adjusts itself therefore towards parallel conditions, the chief variation being in the relative proportions of the two races and the details of the methods by which black labour is made to serve white ends.

In these black and white communities which are establishing themselves in all those parts of the earth where once the black was native, or in which a sub-tropical climate is favourable to his existence at a low level of social development, there is – and there is bound to be for many years to come – much racial tension. The steady advance of birth-control may mitigate the biological factors of this tension later on, and a general amelioration of manners and conduct may efface that disposition to persecute dissimilar types, which man shares with many other gregarious animals. But meanwhile this tension increases and a vast multitude of lives is strained to tragic issues.

To exaggerate the dangers and evils of miscegenation is a weakness of our time. Man interbreeds with all his varieties and yet deludes himself that there are races of outstanding purity, the "Nordic," the "Semitic," and so forth. These are phantoms of the imagination. The reality is more intricate, less dramatic, and grips less easily upon the mind; the phantoms grip only too well and incite to terrible suppressions. Changes in the number of half-breeds and in the proportion of white and coloured are changes of a temporary nature that may become controllable and rectifiable in a few generations. But until this level of civilization is reached, until the colour of a man's skin or the kinks in a woman's hair cease to have the value of shibboleths that involve educational, professional, and social extinction or survival, a black and white community is bound to be continually preoccupied by a standing feud too intimate and persuasive to permit of any long views of the world's destiny.

We come to the conclusion therefore that it is from the more vigorous, varied, and less severely obsessed centres of the Atlantic civilizations in the temperate zone, with their abundant facilities for publication and discussion, their traditions of mental liberty and their immense variety of interacting free types, that the main beginnings of the Open Conspiracy must develop. For the rest of the world, its propaganda, finding but poor nourishment in the local conditions, may retain a missionary quality for many years.

XIII

Resistances And Antagonistic Forces In Our Conscious And Unconscious Selves

We have dealt in the preceding two chapters with great classes and assemblages of human beings as, in the mass, likely to be more or less antagonistic to the Open Conspiracy, and it has been difficult in those chapters to avoid the implication that "we," some sort of circle round the writer, were aloof from these obstructive and hostile multitudes, and ourselves entirely identified with the Open Conspiracy. But neither are these multitudes so definitely against, nor those who are with us so entirely for, the Open Conspiracy to establish a world community as the writer, in his desire for clearness and contrast and with an all too human disposition perhaps towards plain ego-centred combative issues, has been led to represent. There is no 'we,' and there can be no "we," in possession of the Open Conspiracy.

The Open Conspiracy is in partial possession of us, and we attempt to serve it. But the Open Conspiracy is a natural and necessary development of contemporary thought arising here, there, and everywhere. There are doubts and sympathies that weigh on the side of the Open Conspiracy in nearly everyone, and not one of us but retains many impulses, habits, and ideas in conflict with our general devotion, checking and limiting our service.

Let us therefore in this chapter cease to discuss classes and types and consider general mental tendencies and reactions which move through all humanity.

In our opening chapters we pointed out that religion is not universally distributed throughout human society. And of no one does it seem to have complete possession. It seizes upon some of us and exalts us for one hour now and then, for a day now and then; it may leave its afterglow upon our conduct for some time; it may establish restraints and habitual dispositions; sometimes it dominates us with but brief intermissions through long spells, and then we can be saints and martyrs. In all our religious phases there appears a desire to *hold* the phase, to subdue the rest of our life to the standards and exigencies of that phase. Our quickened intelligence sets itself to a general analysis of our conduct and to the problem of establishing controls over our unilluminated intervals.

And when the religious elements in the mind set themselves to such self-analysis, and attempt to order and unify the whole being upon this basis of the service and advancement of the race, they discover first a great series of indifferent moods, wherein the resistance to thought and word for the Open Conspiracy is merely passive and in the nature of inertia. There is a whole class of states of mind which may be brought together under the head of "everydayism." The dinner bell and the playing fields, the cinema and the newspaper, the week-end visit and the factory siren, a host of such expectant things calls to a vast majority of people in our modern world to stop thinking and get busy with the interest in hand, and so on to the next, without a thought for the general frame and drama in which these momentary and personal incidents are set. We are driven along these marked and established routes and turned this way or that by the accidents of upbringing, of rivalries and loves, of chance encounters and vivid experiences, and it is rarely for many of us, and never for some, that the phases of broad reflection and self-questioning arise. For many people the religious life now, as in the past, has been a quite desperate effort to withdraw sufficient attention and energy from the flood of events to get some sort of grasp, and keep whatever grip is won, upon the relations of the self to the whole. Far more recoil in terror from such a possibility and would struggle strenuously against solitude in the desert, solitude under the stars, solitude in a silent room or indeed any occasion for comprehensive thought.

But the instinct and purpose of the religious type is to keep hold upon the comprehensive drama, and at the heart of all the great religions of the world we find a parallel disposition to escape in some manner from the aimless drive and compulsion of accident and everyday. Escape is attempted either by withdrawal from the presence of crowding circumstance into a mystical contemplation and austere retirement, or – what is more difficult and desperate and reasonable – by imposing the mighty standards of enduring issues upon the whole mass of transitory problems which constitute the actual business of life. We have already noted how the modern mind turns from retreat as a recognizable method of religion, and faces squarely up to the second alternative. The tumult of life has to be met and conquered. Aim must prevail over the aimless. Remaining in normal life we must yet keep our wills and thoughts aloof from normal life and fixed upon creative processes. However busied we may be, however challenged, we must yet save something of our best mental activity for self-examination and keep ourselves alert against the endless treacheries within that would trip us back into everydayism and disconnected responses to the stimuli of life.

Religions in the past, though they have been apt to give a preference to the renunciation of things mundane, have sought by a considerable variety of expedients to preserve the faith of those whom chance or duty still kept in normal contact with the world. It would provide material for an interesting study to enquire how its organizations to do this have worked in the past and how far they may be imitated and paralleled in the progressive life of the future. All the wide-reaching religions which came into existence in the five centuries before and the five centuries after Christ have made great use of periodic meetings for mutual reassurance, of sacred books, creeds, fundamental heart-searchings, of confession, prayer, sacraments, seasons of withdrawal, meditation, fasting, and prayer. Do these methods mark a phase in the world's development, or are they still to be considered available?

This points to a very difficult tangle of psychological problems. The writer in his earlier draft of this book wrote that the modern religious individual leads, spiritually speaking, a life of extreme wasteful and dangerous isolation. He still feels that is true, but he realizes that the invention of corrective devices is not within his range. He cannot picture a secular Mass nor congregations singing hymns about the Open Conspiracy. Perhaps the modern soul in trouble will resort to the psychoanalysts instead of the confessional; in which case we need to pray for better psychoanalysts.

Can the modern mind work in societies? May the daily paper be slowly usurping the functions of morning prayer, a daily mental reminder of large things, with more vividness and, at present, lower standards? One of the most distressful facts of the spread of education in the nineteenth century was the unscrupulous exploitation of the new reading public by a group of trash-dealers who grew rich and mighty in the process. Is the popular publisher and newspaper proprietor always to remain a trash-dealer? Or are we to see, in the future, publications taking at times some or all of the influence of revivalist movements, and particular newspapers rising to the task of sustaining a common faith in a gathering section of the public ?

The modern temple in which we shall go to meditate may be a museum; the modern religious house and its religious life may be a research organization. The Open Conspirator must see to it that the museums show their meaning plain. There may be not only literature presently, but even plays, shows, and music, to subserve new ideas instead of trading upon tradition.

It is plain that to read and be moved by great ideas and to form good resolutions with no subsequent reminders and moral stocktaking is not enough to keep people in the way of the Open Conspiracy. The relapse to everydayism is too easy. The contemporary Open Conspirator may forget, and he has nothing to remind him; he may relapse, and he will hear no reproach to warn him of his relapse. Nowhere has he recorded a vow. "Everyday" has endless ways of justifying the return of the believer to sceptical casualness. It is easy to persuade oneself that one is taking life or oneself "too seriously." The mind is very self-protective; it has a disposition to abandon too great or too far-reaching an effort and return to things indisputably within its scope. We have an instinctive preference for thinking things are "all right"; we economize anxiety; we defend the delusions that we can work with, even though we half realize they are no more than delusions. We resent the warning voice, the critical question that robs our activities of assurance. Our everyday moods are not only the antagonists of our religious moods, but they resent all outward appeals to our religious moods, and they welcome every help against religious appeals. We pass very readily from the merely defensive to the defensive-aggressive, and from refusing to hear the word that might stir our consciences to a vigorous effort to suppress its utterance.

Churches, religious organizations, try to keep the revivifying phase and usage where it may strike upon the waning or slumbering faith of the convert, but modern religion as yet has no such organized reminders. They cannot be improvised. Crude attempts to supply the needed corrective of conduct may do less good than harm. Each one of us for himself must do what he can to keep his high resolve in mind and protect himself from the snare of his own moods of fatigue or inadvertency.

But these passive and active defences of current things which operate in and through ourselves, and find such ready sympathy and assistance in the world about us, these massive resistance systems, are only the beginning of our tale of the forces antagonistic to the Open Conspiracy that lurk in our complexities.

Men are creatures with other faults quite beyond and outside our common disposition to be stupid, indolent, habitual, and defensive. Not only have we active creative impulses, but also acutely destructive ones. Man is a jealous animal. In youth and adolescence egotism is extravagant. It is natural for it to be extravagant, then, and there is no help for it. A great number of us at that stage would rather not see a beautiful or wonderful thing come into existence than have it come into existence disregarding us. Something of that jealous malice, that self-assertive ruthlessness, remains in all of us throughout life. At his worst man can be an exceedingly combative, malignant, mischievous and cruel animal. None of us are altogether above the possibility of such phases. When we consider the oppositions to the Open Conspiracy that operate in the normal personality, we appreciate the soundness of the catechism which instructs us to renounce not only the trivial world and the heavy flesh, but the active and militant devil.

To make is a long and wearisome business, with many arrests and disappointments, but to break gives an instant thrill. We all know something of the delight of the *Bang*. It is well for the Open Conspirator to ask himself at times how far he is in love with the dream of a world in order, and how far he is driven by hatred of institutions that bore or humiliate him. He may be no more than a revengeful incendiary in the mask of a constructive worker. How safe is he, then, from the reaction to some fresh humiliation? The Open Conspiracy which is now his refuge and vindication may presently fail to give him the compensation he has sought, may offer him no better than a minor role, may display irritating and incomprehensible preferences. And for a great number of things in overt antagonism to the great aim of the Open Conspiracy, he will still find within himself not simply acquiescence but sympathy and a genuine if inconsistent admiration. There they are, waiting for his phase of disappointment. Back he may go to the old loves with a new animus against the greater scheme. He may be glad to be quit of prigs and humbugs, and back among the good fellowship of nothing in particular.

Man has pranced a soldier in reality and fancy for so many generations that few of us can altogether release our imaginations from the brilliant pretensions of flags, empire, patriotism, and aggression. Business men, especially in America, seem to feel a sort of glory in calling even the underselling and overadvertising of rival enterprises "fighting." Pill vendors and public departments can have their "wars," their heroisms, their desperate mischiefs, and so get that Napoleonic feeling. The world and our reveries are full of the sentimentalities, the false glories and loyalties of the old combative traditions, trailing after them, as they do, so much worth and virtue in a dulled and stupefied condition. It is difficult to resist the fine gravity, the high self-respect, the examples of honour and good style in small things, that the military and naval services can present to us, for all that they are now no more than noxious parasites upon the nascent world commonweal. In France not a word may be said against the army; in England, against the navy. There will be many Open Conspirators at first who will scarcely dare to say that word even to themselves.

But all these obsolete values and attitudes with which our minds are cumbered must be cleared out if the new faith is to have free play. We have to clear them out not only from our own minds but from the minds of others who are to become our associates. The finer and more picturesque these obsolescent loyalties, obsolescent standards of honour, obsolescent religious associations, may seem to us, the more thoroughly must we seek to release our minds and the minds of those about us from them and cut off all thoughts of a return.

We cannot compromise with these vestiges of the ancient order and be faithful servants of the new. Whatever we retain of them will come back to life and grow again. It is no good to operate for cancer unless the whole growth is removed. Leave a crown about and presently you will find it being worn by someone resolved to be a king. Keep the name and image of a god without a distinct museum label and sooner or later you will discover a worshipper on his knees to it and be lucky not to find a human sacrifice upon the altar. Wave a flag and it will wrap about you. Of yourself even more than of the community is this true; there can be no half measures. You have not yet completed your escape to the Open Conspiracy from the cities of the plain while it is still possible for you to take a single backward glance.

XIV

THE OPEN CONSPIRACY BEGINS AS A MOVEMENT OF DISCUSSION, EXPLANATION, AND PROPAGANDA

A new and happier world, a world community, is awakening, within the body of the old order, to the possibility of its emergence. Our phrase, "the Open Conspiracy" is merely a name for that awakening. To begin with, the Open Conspiracy is necessarily a group of ideas.

It is a system of modern ideas which has been growing together in the last quarter of the century, and particularly since the war. It is the reaction of a rapidly progressing biological conception of life and of enlarged historical realizations upon the needs and urgencies of the times. In this book we are attempting to define this system and to give it this provisional name. Essentially at first it is a dissemination of this new ideology that must occur. The statement must be tried over and spread before a widening circle of people.

Since the idea of the Open Conspiracy rests upon and arises out of a synthesis of historical, biological, and sociological realizations, we may look for these realizations already in the case of people with sound knowledge in these fields; such people will be prepared for acquiescence without any explanatory work; there is nothing to set out to them beyond the suggestion that it is time they became actively conscious of where they stand. They constitute already the Open Conspiracy in an unorganized solution, and they will not so much adhere as admit to themselves and others their state of mind. They will say, "We knew all that." Directly we pass beyond that comparatively restricted world, however, we find that we have to deal with partial knowledge, with distorted views, or with blank ignorance, and that a revision and extension of historical and biological ideas and a considerable elucidation of economic misconceptions have to be undertaken. Such people have to be brought up to date with their information.

I have told already how I have schemed out a group of writings to embody the necessary ideas of the new time in a form adapted to the current reading public; I have made a sort of provisional "Bible," so to speak, for some factors at least in the Open Conspiracy. It is an early sketch. As the current reading public changes, all this work will become obsolescent so far as its present form and method go. But not so far as its substantial method goes. That I believe will remain.

Ultimately this developing mass of biological, historical, and economic information and suggestion must be incorporated in general education if the Open Conspiracy is to come to its own. At present this propaganda has to go on among adolescents and adults because of the backwardness and political conservatism of existing educational organizations. Most real modern education now is done in spite of the schools and to correct the misconceptions established by the schools. But what will begin as adult propaganda must pass into a *kultur-kampf* to win our educational machinery from reaction and the conservation of outworn ideas and attitudes to the cause of world reconstruction. The Open Conspiracy itself can never be imprisoned and fixed in the form of an organization, but everywhere Open Conspirators should be organizing themselves for educational reform.

And also within the influence of this comprehensive project there will be all sorts of groupings for study and progressive activity. One can presuppose the formation of groups of friends, of family groups, of students and employees or other sorts of people, meeting and conversing frequently in the course of their normal occupations, who will exchange views and find themselves in agreement upon this idea of a constructive change of the world as the guiding form of human activities.

Fundamentally important issues upon which unanimity must be achieved from the outset are:

Firstly, the entirely provisional nature of all existing governments, and the entirely provisional nature, therefore, of all loyalties associated therewith;

Secondly, the supreme importance of population control in human biology and the possibility it affords us of a release from the pressure of the struggle for existence on ourselves; and

Thirdly, the urgent necessity of protective resistance against the present traditional drift towards war.

People who do not grasp the vital significance of these test issues do not really begin to understand the Open Conspiracy. Groups coming into agreement upon these matters, and upon their general interpretation of history, will be in a position to seek adherents, enlarge themselves, and attempt to establish communication and co-operation with kindred groups for common ends. They can take up a variety of activities to develop a sense and habit of combined action and feel their way to greater enterprises.

We have seen already that the Open Conspiracy must be heterogeneous in origin. Its initial groupings and associations will be of no uniform pattern. They will be of a very different size, average age, social experience, and influence. Their particular activities will be determined by these things. Their diverse qualities and influences will express themselves by diverse attempts at organization, each effective in its own sphere. A group or movement of students may find itself capable of little more than self education and personal propaganda; a handful of middle-class people in a small town may find its small resources fully engaged at first in such things as, for example, seeing that desirable literature is available for sale or in the local public library, protecting books and news vendors from suppression, or influencing local teachers. Most parents of school children can press for the teaching of universal history and sound biology and protest against the inculcation of aggressive patriotism. There is much scope for the single individual in this direction. On the other hand, a group of ampler experience and resources may undertake the printing, publication, and distribution of literature, and exercise considerable influence upon public opinion in turning education in the right direction. The League of Nations movement, the Birth Control movement, and most radical and socialist societies, are fields into which Open Conspirators may go to find adherents more than half prepared for their wider outlook. The Open Conspiracy is a fuller and ampler movement into which these incomplete activities must necessarily merge as its idea takes possession of men's imaginations.

From the outset, the Open Conspiracy will set its face against militarism. There is a plain present need for the organization now, before war comes again, of an open and explicit refusal to serve in any war – or at most to serve in war, directly or indirectly, only after the issue has been fully and fairly submitted to arbitration. The time for a conscientious objection to war service is manifestly before and not after the onset of war. People who have by their silence acquiesced in a belligerent foreign policy right up to the onset of war, have little to complain of if they are then compelled to serve. And a refusal to participate with one's country in warfare is a preposterously incomplete gesture unless it is rounded off by the deliberate advocacy of a world pax, a world economic control, and a restrained population, such as the idea of the Open Conspiracy embodies.

The putting upon record of its members' reservation of themselves from any or all of the military obligations that may be thrust upon the country by military and diplomatic effort, might very conceivably be the first considerable overt act of many Open Conspiracy groups. It would supply the practical incentive to bring many of them together in the first place. It would necessitate the creation of regional or national *ad hoc* committees for the establishment of a collective legal and political defensive for this dissent from current militant nationalism. It would bring the Open Conspiracy very early out of the province of discussion into the field of practical conflict. It would from the outset invest it with a very necessary quality of present applicability.

The anticipatory repudiation of military service, so far as this last may be imposed by existing governments in their factitious international rivalries, need not necessarily involve a denial of the need of military action on behalf of the world commonweal for the suppression of nationalist brigandage, nor need it prevent the military training of Open Conspirators. It is simply the practical form of assertion that the normal militant diplomacy and warfare of the present time are offences against civilization, processes in the nature of brigandage, sedition, and civil war, and that serious men cannot be expected to play anything but a role of disapproval, non-participation, or active prevention towards them. Our loyalty to our current government, we would intimate, is subject to its sane and adult behaviour.

These educational and propagandist groups drawing together into an organized resistance to militarism and to the excessive control of individuals by the makeshift governments of to-day, constitute at most only the earliest and more elementary grade of the Open Conspiracy, and we will presently go on to consider the more specialized and constructive forms its effort must evoke. Before doing so, however, we may say a little more about the structure and method of these possible initiatory groupings.

Since they are bound to be different and miscellaneous in form, size, quality, and ability, any early attempts to organize them into common general action or even into regular common gatherings are to be deprecated. There should be many types of groups. Collective action had better for a time – perhaps for a long time – be undertaken not through the merging of groups but through the formation of *ad hoc* associations for definitely specialized ends, all making for the new world civilization. Open Conspirators will come into these associations to make a contribution very much as people come into limited liability companies, that is to say with a subscription and not with their whole capital. A comprehensive organization attempting from the first to cover all activities would necessarily rest upon and promote one prevalent pattern of activity and hamper or estrange the more original and interesting forms. It would develop a premature orthodoxy, it would cease almost at once to be creative, and it would begin to form a crust of tradition. It would become anchylosed. With the dreadful examples of Christianity and Communism before us, we must insist that the idea of the Open Conspiracy ever becoming a single organization must be dismissed from the mind. It is a movement, yes, a system of purposes, but its end is a free and living, if unified, world.

At the utmost seven broad principles may be stated as defining the Open Conspiracy and holding it together. And it is possible even of these, one, the seventh, may be, if not too restrictive, at least unnecessary. To the writer it seems unavoidable because it is so intimately associated with that continual dying out of tradition upon which our hopes for an unencumbered and expanding human future rest.

(1) The complete assertion, practical as well as theoretical, of the provisional nature of existing governments and of our acquiescence in them;

(2) The resolve to minimize by all available means the conflicts of these governments, their militant use of individuals and property, and their interferences with the establishment of a world economic system;

(3) The determination to replace private, local or national ownership of at

least credit, transport, and staple production by a responsible world directorate serving the common ends of the race;

(4) The practical recognition of the necessity for world biological controls, for example, of population and disease;

(5) The support of a minimum standard of individual freedom and welfare in the world; and

(6) The supreme duty of subordinating the personal career to the creation of a world directorate capable of these tasks and to the general advancement of human knowledge, capacity, and power;

(7) The admission therewith that our immortality is conditional and lies in the race and not in our individual selves.

XV

EARLY CONSTRUCTIVE WORK OF THE OPEN CONSPIRACY

In such terms we may sketch the practicable and possible opening phase of the Open Conspiracy.

We do not present it as a movement initiated by any individual or radiating from any particular centre. In this book we are not starting something; we are describing and participating in something which has started. It arises naturally and necessarily from the present increase of knowledge and the broadening outlook of many minds throughout the world, and gradually it becomes conscious of itself. It is reasonable therefore to anticipate its appearance all over the world in sporadic mutually independent groupings and movements, and to recognize not only that they will be extremely various, but that many of them will trail with them racial and regional habits and characteristics which will only be shaken off as its cosmopolitan character becomes imperatively evident.

The passage from the partial anticipations of the Open Conspiracy that already abound everywhere to its complete and completely self-conscious statement may be made by almost imperceptible degrees. To-day it may seem no more than a visionary idea; to-morrow it may be realized as a world-wide force of opinion and will. People will pass with no great inconsistency from saying that the Open Conspiracy is impossible to saying that it has always been plain and clear to them, that to this fashion they have shaped their lives as long as they can remember.

In its opening phase, in the day of small things, quite minor accidents may help or delay the clear definition and popularization of its main ideas. The changing pattern of public events may disperse or concentrate attention upon it, or it may win the early adherence of men of exceptional resources, energy, or ability. It is impossible to foretell the speed of its advance. Its development may be slower or faster, direct or devious, but the logic of accumulating realizations thrusts it forward, will persist in thrusting it on, and sooner or later it will be discovered, conscious and potent, the working religion of most sane and energetic people.

Meanwhile our supreme virtues must be faith and persistence.

So far we have considered only two of the main activities of the Open

Conspiracy, the one being its propaganda of confidence in the possible world commonweal, and the other its immediate practical attempt to systematize resistance to militant and competitive imperialism and nationalism. But such things are merely its groundwork undertakings; they do no more than clear the site and make the atmosphere possible for its organized constructive efforts.

Directly we turn to that, we turn to questions of special knowledge, special effort, and special organization.

Let us consider first the general advancement of science, the protection and support of scientific research, and the diffusion of scientific knowledge These things fall within the normal scheme of duty for the members of the Open Conspiracy. The world of science and experiment is the region of origin of nearly all the great initiatives that characterize our times; the Open Conspiracy owes its inspiration, its existence, its form and direction entirely to the changes of condition these initiatives have brought about, and yet a large number of scientific workers live outside the sphere of sympathy in which we may expect the Open Conspiracy to materialize, and collectively their political and social influence upon the community is extraordinarily small. Having regard to the immensity of its contributions and the incalculable value of its promise to the modern community, science – research, that is, and the diffusion of scientific knowledge – is extraordinarily neglected, starved, and threatened by hostile interference. This is largely because scientific work has no strong unifying organization and cannot in itself develop such an organization.

Science is a hard mistress, and the first condition of successful scientific work is that the scientific man should stick to his research. The world of science is therefore in itself, at its core, a miscellany of specialists, often very ungracious specialists, and, rather than offer him help and co-operation, it calls for understanding, tolerance, and service from the man of more general intelligence and wider purpose. The company of scientific men is less like a host of guiding angels than like a swarm of marvellous bees – endowed with stings – which must be hived and cherished and multiplied by the Open Conspiracy.

But so soon as we have the Open Conspiracy at work, putting its case plainly and offering its developing ideas and activities to those most preciously preoccupied men, then reasonably, when it involves no special trouble for them, when it is the line of least resistance for them, they may be expected to fall in with its convenient and helpful aims and find in it what they have hitherto lacked, a common system of political and social concepts to hold them together.

When that stage is reached, we shall be saved such spectacles of intellectual prostitution as the last Great War offered, when men of science were herded blinking from their laboratories to curse one another upon nationalist lines, and when after the war stupid and wicked barriers were set up to the free communication of knowledge by the exclusion of scientific men of this or that nationality from international scientific gatherings. The Open Conspiracy must help the man of science to realize, what at present he fails most astonishingly to realize, that he belongs to a greater comity than any king or president represents to-day, and so prepare him for better behaviour in the next season of trial.

The formation of groups in, and not only in, but about and in relation to, the scientific world, which will add to those first main activities of the Open Conspiracy, propaganda and pacificism, a special attention to the needs of scientific work, may be enlarged upon with advantage here, because it will illustrate quite typically the idea of a special work carried on in relation to a general activity, which is the subject of this section.

The Open Conspiracy extends its invitation to all sorts and conditions of men, but the service of scientific progress is for those only who are specially equipped or who are sufficiently interested to equip themselves. For scientific work there is first of all a great need of endowment and the setting up of laboratories, observatories, experimental stations, and the like, in all parts of the world. Numbers of men and women capable of scientific work never achieve it for want of the stimulus of opportunity afforded by endowment. Few contrive to create their own opportunities. The essential man of science is very rarely an able collector or administrator of money, and anyhow, the detailed work of organization is a grave call upon his special mental energy. But many men capable of a broad and intelligent appreciation of scientific work, but not capable of the peculiar intensities of research, have the gift of extracting money from private and public sources, and it is for them to use that gift modestly and generously in providing the framework for those more especially endowed.

And there is already a steadily increasing need for the proper storage and indexing of scientific results, and every fresh worker enhances it. Quite a considerable amount of scientific work goes fruitless or is needlessly repeated because of the growing volume of publication, and men make discoveries in the field of reality only to lose them again in the lumber room of record. Here is a second line of activity to which the Open Conspirator with a scientific bias may direct his attention.

A third line is the liaison work between the man of science and the common intelligent man; the promotion of publications which will either state the substance, implications; and consequences of new work in the vulgar tongue, or, if that is impossible, train the general run of people to the new idioms and technicalities which need to be incorporated with the vulgar tongue if it is still to serve its ends as a means of intellectual intercourse.

Through special *ad hoc* organizations, societies for the promotion of Research, for Research Defence, for World Indexing, for the translation of Scientific Papers, for the Diffusion of New Knowledge, the surplus energies of a great number of Open Conspirators can be directed to entirely creative ends and a new world system of scientific work built up, within which such dear old institutions as the Royal Society of London, the various European Academies of Science and the like, now overgrown and inadequate, can maintain their

117

venerable pride in themselves, their mellowing prestige, and their distinguished exclusiveness, without their present privilege of inflicting cramping slights and restrictions upon the more abundant scientific activities of to-day.

So in relation to science – and here the word is being used in its narrower accepted meaning for what is often spoken of as *pure* science, the search for physical and biological realities, uncomplicated by moral, social, and "practical" considerations – we evoke a conception of the Open Conspiracy as producing groups of socially associated individuals, who engage primarily in the general basic activities of the Conspiracy and adhere to and promote the seven broad principles summarized at the end of Chapter Fourteen, but who work also with the larger part of their energies, through international and cosmopolitan societies and in a multitude of special ways, for the establishment of an enduring and progressive world organization of pure research. They will have come to this special work because their distinctive gifts, their inclinations, their positions and opportunities have indicated it as theirs.

Now a very parallel system of Open Conspiracy groups is conceivable, in relation to business and industrial life. It would necessarily be a vastly bulkier and more heterogeneous system of groups, but otherwise the analogy is complete. Here we imagine those people whose gifts, inclinations, positions and opportunities as directors, workers, or associates give them an exceptional insight into and influence in the processes of producing and distributing commodities, can also be drawn together into groups within the Open Conspiracy. But these groups will be concerned with the huge and more complicated problems of the processes by which even now the small isolated individual adventures in production and trading that constituted the economic life of former civilizations, are giving place to larger, better instructed, better planned industrial organizations, whose operations and combinations become at last world wide.

The amalgamations and combinations, the substitution of large-scale business for multitudes of small-scale businesses, which are going on now, go on with all the cruelty and disregards of a natural process. If a man is to profit and survive, these unconscious blunderings – which now stagger towards but which may never attain world organization – much be watched, controlled, mastered, and directed. As uncertainty diminishes, the quality of adventure and the amount of waste diminish also, and large speculative profits are no longer possible or justifiable. The transition from speculative adventure to organized foresight in the common interest, in the whole world of economic life, is the substantial task of the Open Conspiracy. And it is these specially interested and equipped groups, and not the movement as a whole, which may best begin the attack upon these fundamental readjustments.

The various Socialist movements of the nineteenth and earlier twentieth centuries had this in common, that they sought to replace the "private owner" in most or all economic interests by some vaguely apprehended "public owner". This, following the democratic disposition of the times, was commonly conceived of as an elected body, a municipality, the parliamentary state or what not. There were municipal socialists, "nationalizing" socialists, imperial socialists. In the mystic teachings of the Marxist, the collective owner was to be "the dictatorship of the proletariat." Production for profit was denounced. The contemporary mind realizes the evils of production for profit and of the indiscriminate scrambling of private ownership more fully than ever before, but it has a completer realization and a certain accumulation of experience in the difficulties of organizing that larger ownership we desire. Private ownership may not be altogether evil as a provisional stage, even if it has no more in its favour than the ability to transcend political boundaries.

Moreover – and here again the democratic prepossessions of the nineteenth century come in – the Socialist movements sought to make every single adherent a reformer and a propagandist of economic methods. In order to do so, it was necessary to simplify economic processes to the crudity of nursery toys, and the intricate interplay of will and desire in enterprise, normal employment, and direction, in questions of ownership, wages, credit, and money, was reduced to a childish fable of surplus value wickedly appropriated. The Open Conspiracy is not so much a socialism as a more comprehensive offspring which has eaten and assimilated whatever was digestible of its socialist forbears. It turns to biology for guidance towards the regulation of quantity and a controlled distribution of the human population of the world, and it judges all the subsidiary aspects of property and pay by the criterion of most efficient production and distribution in relation to the indications thus obtained.

These economic groups, then, of the Open Conspiracy, which may come indeed to be a large part of the Open Conspiracy, will be working in that vast task of economic reconstruction – which from the point of view of the older socialism was the sole task before mankind. They will be conducting experiments and observing processes according to their opportunities. Through *ad hoc* societies and journals they will be comparing and examining their methods and preparing reports and clear information for the movement at large. The whole question of money and monetary methods in our modern communities, so extraordinarily disregarded in socialist literature, will be examined under the assumption that money is the token of the community's obligation, direct or indirect, to an individual, and credit its permission to deal freely with material.

The whole psychology of industry and industrial relationship needs to be revised and restated in terms of the collective efficiency and welfare of mankind. And just as far as can be contrived, the counsel and the confidences of those who now direct great industrial and financial operations will be invoked. The first special task of a banker, or a bank clerk for that matter, who joins the Open Conspiracy, will be to answer the questions: "What is a bank?" "What are you going to do about it?" "What have we to do about it?" The first questions to a manufacturer will be: "What are you making and why?" and

"What are you and we to do about it?" Instead of the crude proposals to "expropriate" and "take over by the State" of the primitive socialism, the Open Conspiracy will build up an encyclopaedic conception of the modern economic complex as a labyrinthine pseudo-system progressively eliminating waste and working its way along multitudinous channels towards unity, towards clarity of purpose and method, towards abundant productivity and efficient social service.

Let us come back now for a paragraph or so to the ordinary adherent to the Open Conspiracy, the adherent considered not in relation to his special aptitudes and services, but in relation to the movement as a whole and to those special constructive organizations outside his own field. It will be his duty to keep his mind in touch with the progressing concepts of the scientific work so far as he is able and with the larger issues of the economic reconstruction that is afoot, to take his cues from the special groups and organizations engaged upon that work, and to help where he finds his opportunity and when there is a call upon him. But no adherent of the Open Conspiracy can remain merely and completely an ordinary adherent. There can be no pawns in the game of the Open Conspiracy, no "cannon fodder" in its war. A special activity, quite as much as a general understanding, is demanded from everyone who looks creatively towards the future of mankind.

We have instanced first the fine and distinctive world organization of pure science, and then the huge massive movement towards co-operating unity of aim in the economic life, until at last the production and distribution of staple necessities is apprehended as one world business, and we have suggested that this latter movement may gradually pervade and incorporate a very great bulk of human activities. But besides this fine current and this great torrent of evolving activities and relationships there are also a very considerable variety of other great functions in the community towards which Open Conspiracy groups must direct their organizing enquiries and suggestions in their common intention of ultimately assimilating all the confused processes of to-day into a world community.

For example, there must be a series of groups in close touch at one end with biological science and at the other with the complex of economic activity, who will be concerned specially with the practical administration of the biological interests of the race, from food plants and industrial products to pestilences and population. And another series of groups will gather together attention and energy to focus them upon the educational process. We have already pointed out that there is a strong disposition towards conservatism in normal educational institutions. They preserve traditions rather than develop them. They are likely to set up a considerable resistance to the reconstruction of the world outlook upon the threefold basis defined in Chapter Fourteen. This resistance must be attacked by special societies, by the establishment of competing schools, by help and promotion for enlightened teachers, and, wherever the attack is incompletely successful, it must be supplemented by the energetic diffusion of educational literature for adults, upon modern lines. The forces of the entire movement may be mobilized in a variety of ways to bring pressure upon reactionary schools and institutions.

A set of activities correlated with most of the directly creative ones will lie through existing political and administrative bodies. The political work of the Open Conspiracy must be conducted upon two levels and by entirely different methods. Its main political idea, its political strategy, is to weaken, efface, incorporate, or supersede existing governments. But there is also a tactical diversion of administrative powers and resources to economic and educational arrangements of a modern type. Because a country or a district is inconvenient as a division and destined to ultimate absorption in some more comprehensive and economical system of government, that is no reason why its administration should not be brought meanwhile into working cooperation with the development of the Open Conspiracy. Free Trade nationalism in power is better than high tariff nationalism, and pacificist party liberalism better than aggressive party patriotism.

This evokes the anticipation of another series of groups, a group in every possible political division, whose task it will be to organize the whole strength of the Open Conspiracy in that division as an effective voting or agitating force. In many divisions this might soon become a sufficiently considerable block to affect the attitudes and pledges of the national politicians. The organization of these political groups into provincial or national conferences and systems would follow hard upon their appearance. In their programmes they would be guided by meetings and discussions with the specifically economic, educational, biological, scientific and central groups, but they would also form their own special research bodies to work out the incessant problems of transition between the old type of locally centred administrations and a developing world system of political controls.

In the preceding chapter we sketched the first practicable first phase of the Open Conspiracy as the propaganda of a group of interlocking ideas, a propaganda associated with pacificist action. In the present chapter we have given a scheme of branching and amplifying development. In this scheme, this scheme of the second phase, we conceive of the Open Conspiracy as consisting of a great multitude and variety of overlapping groups, but now all organized for collective political, social, and educational as well as propagandist action. They will recognize each other much more clearly than they did at first, and they will have acquired a common name.

The groups, however, almost all of them, will still have specific work also. Some will be organizing a sounder setting for scientific progress, some exploring new social and educational possibilities, many concentrated upon this or that phase in the reorganization of the world's economic life, and so forth. The individual Open Conspirator may belong to one or more groups and in addition to the *ad hoc* societies and organizations which the movement will sustain, often in co-operation with partially sympathetic people still outside its ranks.

The character of the Open Conspiracy will now be plainly displayed. It will have become a great world movement as wide-spread and evident as socialism or communism. It will have taken the place of these movements very largely. It will be more than they were, it will be frankly a world religion. This large, loose assimilatory mass of movements, groups, and societies will be definitely and obviously attempting to swallow up the entire population of the world and become the new human community.

XVI

Existing And Developing Movements Which Are Contributory To The Open Conspiracy And Which Must Develop A Common Consciousness. The Parable Of Provinder Island

A suggestion has already been made in an earlier chapter of this essay which may perhaps be expanded here a little more. It is that there already exist in the world a considerable number of movements in industry, in political life, in social matters, in education, which point in the same direction as the Open Conspiracy and are inspired by the same spirit. It will be interesting to discuss how far some of these movements may not become confluent with others and by a mere process of logical completion identify themselves consciously with the Open Conspiracy in its entirety

Consider, for example, the movement for a scientific study and control of population pressure, known popularly as the Birth Control movement. By itself, assuming existing political and economic conditions, this movement lays itself open to the charge of being no better than a scheme of "race suicide." If a population in some area of high civilization attempts to restrict increase, organize its economic life upon methods of maximum individual productivity, and impose order and beauty upon its entire territory, that region will become irresistibly attractive to any adjacent festering mass of low-grade, highly reproductive population. The cheap humanity of the one community will make a constant attack upon the other, affording facile servility, prostitutes, toilers, hand labour. Tariffs against sweated products, restriction of immigration, tensions leading at last to a war of defensive massacre are inevitable. The conquest of an illiterate, hungry, and incontinent multitude may be almost as disastrous as defeat for the selecter race. Indeed, one finds that in discussion the propagandists of Birth Control admit that their project must be universal or dysgenic. But yet quite a number of them do not follow up these admissions to their logical consequences, produce the lines and continue the curves until the complete form of the Open Conspiracy appears. It will be the business of the early Open Conspiracy propagandists to make them do so, and to install groups and representatives at every possible point of vantage in this movement.

And similarly the now very numerous associations for world peace halt in alarm on the edge of their own implications. World Peace remains a vast aspiration until there is some substitute for the present competition of states for markets and raw material, and some restraint upon population pressure. League of Nations Societies and all forms of pacificist organization are either futile or insincere until they come into line with the complementary propositions of the Open Conspiracy.

The various Socialist movements again are partial projects professing at present to be self-sufficient schemes. Most of them involve a pretence that national and political forces are intangible phantoms, and that the primary issue of population pressure can be ignored. They produce one woolly scheme after another for transferring the property in this, that, or the other economic plant and interest from bodies of shareholders and company promoters to gangs of politicians or syndicates of workers – to be steered to efficiency, it would seem, by pillars of cloud by day and pillars of fire by night. The communist party has trained a whole generation of disciples to believe that the overthrow of a vaguely apprehended "Capitalism" is the simple solution of all human difficulties. No movement ever succeeded so completely in substituting phrases for thought. In Moscow communism has trampled "Capitalism" underfoot for ten eventful years, and still finds all the problems of social and political construction before it.

But as soon as the Socialist or Communist can be got to realize that his repudiation of private monopolization is not a complete programme but just a preliminary principle, he is ripe for the ampler concepts of the modern outlook. The Open Conspiracy is the natural inheritor of socialist and communist enthusiasms; it may be in control of Moscow before it is in control of New York.

The Open Conspiracy may achieve the more or less complete amalgamation of all the radical impulses in the Atlantic community of to-day. But its scope is not confined to the variety of sympathetic movements which are brought to mind by that loose word *radical*. In the past fifty years or so, while Socialists and Communists have been denouncing the current processes of economic life in the same invariable phrases and with the same undiscriminating animosity, these processes have been undergoing the profoundest and most interesting changes. While socialist thought has recited its phrases, with witty rather than substantial variations, a thousand times as many clever people have been busy upon industrial, mercantile and financial processes. The Socialist still reiterates that this greater body of intelligence has been merely seeking private gain, which has just as much truth in it as is necessary to make it an intoxicating lie. Everywhere competitive businesses have been giving way to amalgamated enterprises, marching towards monopoly, and personally owned businesses to organizations so large as to acquire more and more the character of publicly responsible bodies. In theory in Great Britain, banks are privately owned, and railway transport is privately owned, and they are run entirely for profit – in practice their profit making is austerely restrained and their proceedings are all the more sensitive to public welfare because they are outside the direct control of party politicians.

Now this transformation of business, trading, and finance has been so multitudinous and so rapid as to be still largely unconscious of itself. Intelligent men have gone from combination to combination and extended their range, year by year, without realizing how their activities were enlarging them to conspicuousness and responsibility. Economic organization is even now only discovering itself for what it is. It has accepted incompatible existing institutions to its own great injury. It has been patriotic and broken its shins against the tariff walls its patriotism has raised to hamper its own movements, it has been imperial and found itself taxed to the limits of its endurance, "controlled" by antiquated military and naval experts, and crippled altogether. The younger, more vigorous intelligences in the great business directorates of to-day are beginning to realize the uncompleted implications of their enterprise. A day will come when the gentlemen who are trying to control the oil supplies of the world without reference to anything else except as a subsidiary factor in their game will be considered to be quaint characters. The ends of Big Business must carry Big Business into the Open Conspiracy just as surely as every other creative and broadly organizing movement is carried.

Now I know that to all this urging towards a unification of constructive effort, a great number of people will be disposed to a reply which will, I hope, be less popular in the future than it is at the present time. They will assume first an expression of great sagacity, an elderly air. Then, smiling gently, they will ask whether there is not something preposterously ambitious in looking at the problem of life as one whole. Is it not wiser to concentrate our forces on more *practicable* things, to attempt one thing at a time, not to antagonize the whole order of established things against our poor desires, to begin tentatively, to refrain from putting too great a strain upon people, to trust to the growing common sense of the world to adjust this or that line of progress to the general scheme of things. Far better accomplish something definite here and there than challenge a general failure. That is, they declare, how reformers and creative things have gone on in the past; that is how they are going on now; muddling forward in a mild and confused and partially successful way. Why not trust them to go on like that? Let each man do his bit with a complete disregard of the logical interlocking of progressive effort to which I have been drawing attention.

Now I must confess that, popular as this style of argument is, it gives me so tedious a feeling that rather than argue against it in general terms I will resort to a parable. I will relate the story of the pig on Provinder Island.

There was, you must understand, only one pig on Provinder Island, and Heaven knows how it got there, whether it escaped and swam ashore or was put ashore from some vessel suddenly converted to vegetarianism, I cannot imagine. At first it was the only mammal there. But later on three sailors and a very small but observant cabin boy were wrecked there, and after subsisting for a time on shell fish and roots they became aware of this pig. And simultaneously they became aware of a nearly intolerable craving for bacon. The eldest of the three sailors began to think of a ham he had met in his boyhood, a beautiful ham for which his father had had the carving knife specially sharpened; the second of the three sailors dreamed repeatedly of a roast loin of pork he had eaten at his sister's wedding, and the third's mind ran on chitterlings – I know not why. They sat about their meagre fire and conferred and expatiated upon these things until their mouths watered and the shell fish turned to water within them. What dreams came to the cabin boy are unknown, for it was their custom to discourage his confidences. But he sat apart brooding and was at last moved to speech. "Let us hunt that old pig," he said, "and kill it."

Now it may have been because it was the habit of these sailors to discourage the cabin boy and keep him in his place, but anyhow, for whatever reason it was, all three sailors set themselves with one accord to oppose that proposal.

"Who spoke of killing the pig?" said the eldest sailor loudly, looking round to see if by any chance the pig was within hearing. "Who spoke of *killing* the pig? You're the sort of silly young devil who jumps at ideas and hasn't no sense of difficulties. What I said was '*AM*. All I want is just a 'Am to go with my roots and sea salt. One 'Am. The Left 'Am. I don't want the right one, and I don't propose to get it. I've got a sense of proportion and a proper share of humour, and I know my limitations. I'm a sound, clear-headed, practical man. 'Am is what I'm after, and if I can get that, I'm prepared to say Quits and let the rest of the pig alone. Who's for joining me in a Left 'Am 'Unt – a simple reasonable Left 'Am 'Unt – just to get One Left 'Am?"

Nobody answered him directly, but when his voice died away, the next sailor in order of seniority took up the tale. "That Boy," he said, "will die of Swelled 'Ed, and I pity him. My idea is to follow up the pig and get hold of a loin chop. Just simply a loin chop. A loin chop is good enough for me. It's – feasible. Much more feasible than a great 'Am. Here we are, we've got no gun, we've got no wood of a sort to make bows and arrows, we've got nothing but our clasp knives, and that pig can run like 'Ell. It's ridiculous to think of killing that pig. But if one didn't trouble him, if one kind of got into his confidence and crept near him and just quietly and insidiously went for his loin just sort of as if one was tickling him – one might get a loin chop almost before he knew of it."

The third sailor sat crumpled up and downcast with his lean fingers tangled in his shock of hair. "Chitterlings," he murmured, "chitterlings. I don't even want to *think* of the pig."

And the cabin boy pursued his own ideas in silence, for he deemed it unwise to provoke his elders further.

On these lines it was the three sailors set about the gratifying of their taste for pork, each in his own way, separately and sanely and modestly. And each had his reward. The first sailor, after weeks of patience, got within arm's length of the pig and smacked that coveted left ham loud and good, and felt success was near. The other two heard the smack and the grunt of dismay half a mile away. But the pig, in a state of astonishment, carried the ham off out of reach, there and then, and that was as close as the first sailor ever got to his objective. The roast loin hunter did no better. He came upon the pig asleep under a rock one day, and jumped upon the very loin he desired, but the pig bit him deeply and septically, and displayed so much resentment that the question of a chop was dropped forthwith and never again broached between them. And thereafter the arm of the second sailor was bandaged and swelled up and went from bad to worse. And as for the third sailor, it is doubtful whether he even got wind of a chitterling from the start to the finish of this parable. The cabin boy, pursuing notions of his own, made a pitfall for the whole pig, but as the others did not help him, and as he was an excessively small – though shrewd – cabin boy, it was a feeble and insufficient pitfall, and all it caught was the hunter of chitterlings, who was wandering distraught. After which the hunter of chitterlings, became a hunter of cabin boys, and the cabin boy's life, for all his shrewdness, was precarious and unpleasant. He slept only in snatches and learned the full bitterness of insight misunderstood.

When at last a ship came to Provinder Island and took off the three men and the cabin boy, the pig was still bacon intact and quite gay and cheerful, and all four castaways were in a very emaciated condition because at that season of the year shell fish were rare, and edible roots were hard to find, and the pig was very much cleverer than they were in finding them and digging them up – let alone digesting them.

From which parable it may be gathered that a partial enterprise is not always wiser or more hopeful than a comprehensive one.

And in the same manner, with myself in the role of that minute but observant cabin boy, I would sustain the proposition that none of these movements of partial reconstruction has the sound common sense quality its supporters suppose. All these movements are worth while if they can be taken into the world-wide movement; all in isolation are futile. They will be overlaid and lost in the general drift. The policy of the whole hog is the best one, the sanest one, the easiest, and the most hopeful. If sufficient men and women of intelligence can realize that simple truth and give up their lives to it, mankind may yet achieve a civilization and power and fullness of life beyond our present dreams. If they do not, frustration will triumph, and war, violence, and a drivelling waste of time and strength and desire, more disgusting even than war, will be the lot of our race down through the ages to its emaciated and miserable end.

For this little planet of ours is quite off the course of any rescue ships, if the will in our species fails.

XVII

THE CREATIVE HOME, SOCIAL GROUP, AND SCHOOL: THE PRESENT WASTE OF IDEALISTIC WILL

Human society began with the family. The natural history of gregarious-ness is a history of the establishment of mutual toleration among human animals, so that a litter or a herd keeps together instead of breaking up. It is in the family group that the restraints, disciplines, and self-sacrifices which make human society possible were worked out and our fundamental prejudices established, and it is in the family group, enlarged perhaps in many respects, and more and more responsive to collective social influences, that our social life must be relearnt, generation after generation.

Now in each generation the Open Conspiracy, until it can develop its own reproductive methods, must remain a minority movement of intelligent converts. A unified progressive world community demands its own type of home and training. It needs to have its fundamental concepts firmly established in as many minds as possible and to guard its children from the infection of the old racial and national hatreds and jealousies, old superstitions and bad mental habits, and base interpretations of life. From its outset the Open Conspiracy will be setting itself to influence the existing educational machinery, but for a long time it will find itself confronted in school and college by powerful religious and political authorities determined to set back the children at the point or even behind the point from which their parents made their escape. At best, the liberalism of the state-controlled schools will be a compromise. Originally schools and colleges were transmitters of tradition and conservative forces. So they remain in essence to this day.

Organized teaching has always aimed, and will always tend to guide, train, and direct, the mind. The problem of reconstructing education so as to make it a releasing instead of a binding process has still to be solved. During the early phases of its struggle, therefore, the Open Conspiracy will be obliged to adopt a certain sectarianism of domestic and social life in the interests of its children, to experiment in novel educational methods and educational atmospheres, and it may even in many cases have to consider the grouping of its families and the establishment of its own schools. In many modern communities, the English-speaking states, for example, there is still liberty to establish educational companies, running schools of a special type. In every country where that right does not exist it has to be fought for.

There lies a great work for various groups of the Open Conspiracy. Successful schools would become laboratories of educational methods and patterns for new state schools. Necessarily for a time, but we may hope unconsciously, the Open Conspiracy children will become a social elite; from their first conscious moments they will begin to think and talk among clear-headed people speaking distinctly and behaving frankly, and it will be a waste and loss to put them back for the scholastic stage among their mentally indistinct and morally muddled contemporaries. A phase when there will be a special educational system for the Open Conspiracy seems, therefore, to be indicated. Its children will learn to speak, draw, think, compute lucidly and subtly, and into their vigorous minds they will take the broad concepts of history, biology, and mechanical progress, the basis of the new world, naturally and easily. Meanwhile, those who grow up outside the advancing educational frontier of the Open Conspiracy will never come under the full influence of its ideas, or they will get hold of them only after a severe struggle against a mass of misrepresentations and elaborately instilled prejudices. An adolescent and adult educational campaign, to undo the fixations and suggestions of the normal conservative and reactionary schools and colleges, is and will long remain an important part of the work of the Open Conspiracy.

Always, as long as I can remember, there have been a dispute and invidious comparisons between the old and the young. The young find the old prey upon and restrain them, and the old find the young shallow, disappointing, and aimless in vivid contrast to their revised memories of their own early days. The present time is one in which these perennial accusations flower with exceptional vigour. But there does seem to be some truth in the statement that the facilities to live frivolously are greater now than they have ever been for old and young alike. For example, in the great modern communities that emerge now from Christendom, there is a widespread disposition to regard Sunday as merely a holiday. But that was certainly not the original intention of Sunday. As we have noted already in an earlier chapter, it was a day dedicated to the greater issues of life. Now great multitudes of people do not even pretend to set aside any time at all to the greater issues of life. The greater issues are neglected altogether. The churches are neglected, and nothing of a unifying or exalting sort takes their place.

What the contemporary senior tells his junior to-day is perfectly correct. In his own youth, no serious impulse of his went to waste. He was not distracted by a thousand gay but petty temptations, and the local religious powers, whatever they happened to be, seemed to believe in themselves more and made a more comprehensive attack upon his conscience and imagination. Now the old faiths are damaged and discredited, and the new and greater one, which is the Open Conspiracy, takes shape only gradually. A decade or so ago, socialism preached its confident hopes, and patriotism and imperial pride shared its attraction for the ever grave and passionate will of emergent youth. Now socialism and democracy are "under revision" and the flags that once waved so bravely reek of poison gas, are stiff with blood and mud and shameful with exposed dishonesties. Youth is what youth has always been, eager for fine interpretations of life, capable of splendid resolves. It has no natural disposition towards the shallow and confused life. Its demand as ever is, "What am I to do with myself?" But it comes up out of its childhood to-day into a world of ruthless exposures and cynical pretensions. We are all a little ashamed of "earnestness." The past ten years have seen the shy and powerful idealism of youth at a loss and dismayed and ashamed as perhaps it has never been before. It is in the world still, but masked, hiding even from itself in a whirl of small excitements and futile, defiant depravities.

The old flags and faiths have lost their magic for the intelligence of the young; they can command it no more; it is in the mighty revolution to which the Open Conspiracy directs itself that the youth of mankind must find its soul, if ever it is to find its soul again.

XVIII

PROGRESSIVE DEVELOPMENT OF THE ACTIVITIES OF THE OPEN CONSPIRACY INTO A WORLD CONTROL AND COMMONWEAL: THE HAZARDS OF THE ATTEMPT

We have now sketched out in these Blue Prints the methods by which the confused radicalism and constructive forces of the present time may, can, and probably will be drawn together about a core of modernized religious feeling into one great and multifarious creative effort. A way has been shown by which this effort may be developed from a mere propagandist campaign and a merely resistant protest against contemporary militarism into an organized fore-shadowing in research, publicity, and experiment in educational, economic, and political reconstructions, of that *Pax Mundi* which has become already the tantalized desire of great multitudes throughout the world. These foreshadowings and reconstructions will ignore and transcend the political boundaries of to-day. They will continually become more substantial as project passes into attempt and performance. In phase after phase and at point after point, therefore, the Open Conspiracy will come to grips with the powers that sustain these boundaries.

And it will not be merely topographical boundaries that will be passed. The Open Conspiracy will also be dissolving and repudiating many existing restrictions upon conduct and many social prejudices. The Open Conspiracy proposes to end and shows how an end may be put to that huge substratum of underdeveloped, undereducated, subjugated, exploited, and frustrated lives upon which such civilization as the world has known hitherto has rested, and upon which most of our social systems still rest.

Whenever possible, the Open Conspiracy will advance by illumination and persuasion. But it has to advance, and even from the outset, where it is not allowed to illuminate and persuade, it must fight. Its first fights will probably be for the right to spread its system of ideas plainly and clearly throughout the world.

There is, I suppose, a flavour of treason about the assumption that any established government is provisional, and a quality of immorality in any criticism of accepted moral standards. Still more is the proposal, made even in times of peace, to resist war levies and conscription an offence against absolute conceptions of loyalty. But the ampler wisdom of the modern Atlantic communities, already touched by premonitions of change and futurity, has continually enlarged the common liberties of thought for some generations, and it is doubtful if there will be any serious resistance to the dissemination of these views and the early organization of the Open Conspiracy in any of the English-speaking communities or throughout the British Empire, in the Scandinavian countries, or in such liberal-minded countries as Holland, Switzerland, republican Germany or France. France, in the hasty years after the war, submitted to some repressive legislation against the discussion of birth control or hostile criticism of the militarist attitude; but such a check upon mental freedom is altogether contrary to the clear and open quality of the French mind; in practice it has already been effectively repudiated by such writers as Victor Margueritte, and it is unlikely that there will be any effective suppression of the opening phases of the Open Conspiracy in France.

This gives us a large portion of the existing civilized world in which men's minds may be readjusted to the idea that their existing governments are in the position of trustees for the greater government of the coming age. Throughout these communities it is conceivable that the structural lines of the world community may be materialized and established with only minor struggles, local boycotts, vigorous public controversies, normal legislative obstruction, social pressure, and overt political activities. Police, jail, expulsions, and so forth, let alone outlawry and warfare, may scarcely be brought into this struggle upon the high civilized level of the Atlantic communities. But where they are brought in, the Open Conspiracy, to the best of its ability and the full extent of its resources, must become a fighting force and organize itself upon resistant lines.

Non-resistance, the restriction of activities to moral suasion is no part of the programme of the Open Conspiracy. In the face of unscrupulous opposition creative ideas must become aggressive, must define their enemies and attack them. By its own organizations or through the police and military strength of governments amenable to its ideas, the movement is bound to find itself fighting for open roads, open frontiers, freedom of speech, and the realities of peace in regions of oppression. The Open Conspiracy rests upon a disrespect for nationality, and there is no reason why it should tolerate noxious or obstructive governments because they hold their own in this or that patch of human territory. It lies within the power of the Atlantic communities to impose peace upon the world and secure unimpeded movement and free speech from end to end of the earth. This is a fact on which the Open Conspiracy must insist. The English-speaking states, France, Germany, Holland, Switzerland, the Scandinavian countries, and Russia, given only a not very extravagant frankness of understanding between them, and a common disposition towards the ideas of the Open Conspiracy, could cease to arm against each other and still exert enough strength to impose disarmament and a respect for human freedom in every corner of the planet. It is fantastic pedantry to wait for all the world to accede before all the world is pacified and policed.

The most inconsistent factor in the liberal and radical thought of to-day is its prejudice against the interference of highly developed modern states in the affairs of less stable and less advanced regions. This is denounced as "imperialism," and regarded as criminal. It may have assumed grotesque and dangerous forms under the now decaying traditions of national competition, but as the merger of the Atlantic states proceeds, the possibility and necessity of bringing areas of misgovernment and disorder under world control increase. A great war like the war of 1914-1918 may never happen again. The common sense of mankind may suffice to avert that. But there is still much actual warfare before mankind, on the frontiers everywhere, against brigands, against ancient loyalties and traditions which will become at last no better than excuses for brigandage and obstructive exaction. All the weight of the Open Conspiracy will be on the side of the world order and against that sort of local independence which holds back its subject people from the citizenship of the world.

But in this broad prospect of far-reaching political amalgamations under the impulses of the Open Conspiracy lurk a thousand antagonisms and adverse chances, like the unsuspected gulleys and ravines and thickets in a wide and distant landscape. We know not what unexpected chasms may presently be discovered. The Open Conspirator may realize that he is one of an advancing and victorious force and still find himself outnumbered and outfought in his own particular corner of the battlefield. No one can yet estimate the possible strength of reaction against world unification; no one can foresee the extent of the divisions and confusions that may arise among ourselves. The ideas in this book may spread about without any serious resistance in most civilized countries, but there are still governments under which the persistent expression of such thoughts will be dealt with as crimes and bring men and women to prison, torment, and death. Nevertheless, they must be expressed.

While the Open Conspiracy is no more than a discussion it may spread unopposed because it is disregarded. As a mainly passive resistance to militarism it may still be tolerable. But as its knowledge and experience accumulate and its organization becomes more effective and aggressive, as it begins to lay hands upon education, upon social habits, upon business developments, as it proceeds to take over the organization of the community, it will marshal not only its own forces but its enemies. A complex of interests will find themselves restrained and threatened by it, and it may easily evoke that most dangerous of human mass feelings, fear. In ways quite unpredictable it may raise a storm against itself beyond all our present imaginings. Our conception of an almost bloodless domination of the Atlantic communities may be merely the confident dream of a thinker whose thoughts have yet to be squarely challenged.

We are not even sure of the common peace. Across the path of mankind the storm of another Great War may break, bringing with it for a time more brutal repressions and vaster injuries even than its predecessor. The scaffoldings and work sheds of the Open Conspiracy may fare violently in that tornado. The restoration of progress may seem an almost hopeless struggle.

It is no part of modern religion to incur needless hardship or go out of the way to seek martyrdom. If we can do our work easily and happily, so it should be done. But the work is not to be shirked because it cannot be done easily and happily. The vision of a world at peace and liberated for an unending growth of knowledge and power is worth every danger of the way. And since in this age of confusion we must live imperfectly and anyhow die, we may as well suffer, if need be, and die for a great end as for none. Never has the translation of vision into realities been easy since the beginning of human effort. The establishment of the world community will surely exact a price – and who can tell what that price may be? – in toil, suffering, and blood.

XIX

HUMAN LIFE IN THE COMING WORLD COMMUNITY

The new life that the Open Conspiracy struggles to achieve through us for our race is first a life of liberations.

The oppression of incessant toil can surely be lifted from everyone, and the miseries due to a great multitude of infections and disorders of nutrition and growth cease to be a part of human experience. Few people are perfectly healthy nowadays except for brief periods of happiness, but the elation of physical well-being will some day be the common lot of mankind.

And not only from natural evils will man be largely free. He will not be left with his soul tangled, haunted by monstrous and irrational fears and a prey to malicious impulse. From his birth he will breathe sweetness and generosity and use his mind and hands cleanly and exactly. He will feel better, will better, think better, see, taste, and hear better than men do now. His undersoul will no longer be a mutinous cavern of ill-treated suppressions and of impulses repressed without understanding. All these releases are plainly possible for him. They pass out of his tormented desire now, they elude and mock him, because chance, confusion, and squalor rule his life. All the gifts of destiny are overlaid and lost to him. He must still suspect and fear. Not one of us is yet as clear and free and happy within himself as most men will some day be. Before mankind lies the prospect not only of health but of magnanimity.

Within the peace and freedom that the Open Conspiracy is winning for us, all these good things that escape us now may be ensured. A graver humanity, stronger, more lovely, longer lived, will learn and develop the ever enlarging possibilities of its destiny. For the first time, the full beauty of this world will be revealed to its unhurried eyes. Its thoughts will be to our thoughts as the thoughts of a man to the troubled mental experimenting of a child. And all the best of us will be living on in that ampler life, as the child and the things it tried and learnt still live in the man. When we were children, we could not think or feel as we think and feel to-day, but to-day we can peer back and still recall something of the ignorances and guesses and wild hopes of these nigh forgotten years.

And so mankind, ourselves still living, but dispersed and reconstructed again in the future, will recall with affection and understanding the desperate wishes and troubled efforts of our present state.

How far can we anticipate the habitations and ways, the usages and adventures, the mighty employments, the ever increasing knowledge and power of the days to come? No more than a child with its scribbling paper and its box of bricks can picture or model the undertakings of its adult years. Our battle is with cruelties and frustrations, stupid, heavy, and hateful things from which we shall escape at last, less like victors conquering a world than like sleepers awaking from a nightmare in the dawn. From any dream, however dismal and horrible, one can escape by realizing that it is a dream, by saying, "I will awake."

The Open Conspiracy is the awaking of mankind from a nightmare, an infantile nightmare, of the struggle for existence and the inevitability of war. The light of day thrusts between our eyelids, and the multitudinous sounds of morning clamour in our ears. A time will come when men will sit with history before them or with some old newspaper before them and ask incredulously, "Was there ever such a world?"

THE END

Index

About the Editor

W. WARREN WAGAR is the Distinguished Teaching Professor of History at Binghamton University, and a Vice President of the H.G. Wells Society. He is the author of several books on Wells.

CPSIA information can be obtained at www.ICGtesting.com
Printed in the USA
LVOW10s0214150414

381738LV00003B/58/P

9 780275 975395